CONCILIU ☑ **W9-ART-334**

DATE DUE

MAR 3 1 2010			
RECEIVED			
APR 1 2 2010			

Demco, Inc. 38-293

CONCILIUM 2005/5

ISLAM AND ENLIGHTENMENT
NEW ISSUES

Edited by

Erik Borgman and Pim Valkenberg

SCM Press · London

BX
1751.2
A1C6
2005/5

c.1

64593718   3-22-06

Published by SCM Press, 9–17 St Albans Place, London N1 0NX

Copyright © Stichting Concilium

English translations copyright © 2005 SCM-Canterbury Press Ltd

All rights reserved. No part of this publication may be
reproduced, stored in a retrieval system, or transmitted,
in any form or by any means, electronic, mechanical, photocopying,
recording or otherwise, without the prior written permission of
Stichting Concilium, Erasmusplein 1,
6525 HT Nijmegen, The Netherlands

ISBN 0 334 03086 2
978 0 334 03086 7

Printed and bound in Great Britain by William Clowes Ltd, Beccles, Suffolk

Concilium Published February, April, June, October
December

Contents

6 *Contents*

Introduction
Islam and Enlightenment – Enlightened Islam – Islam as Enlightening

ERIK BORGMAN AND PIM VALKENBERG

The events of 11 September 2001 have become a worldwide symbol. The images of two aircraft flying into the towers of the World Trade Center in New York, repeated over and over again in the media worldwide, have come to symbolize the supposed threat of aggressive Islam to the peaceful West. The bomb attacks in Madrid on 11 March 2003, and in London on 7 July and 21 July 2005, confirmed to many observers that Samuel Huntington's *Clash of Civilizations* has become reality. There is a professed religious defence of Christian values over against Islam, represented by President George Bush. But the new phenomenon is the polemics against Islam and the way it is currently judged in terms of the liberal Enlightenment and is seriously found wanting.

Recent developments in the Netherlands, some of which made the international headlines, are a case in point. First populist politician Pim Fortuyn broke the taboo on attacking the Muslim faith because it represented a 'backwards culture'. After Fortuyn was murdered on 6 May 2002, this came to be considered as courageous and a long overdue breaking away from a repressing political correctness. Columnist, media personality and film director Theo van Gogh routinely referred to Muslims as to 'geiteneukers' (people having sexual intercourse with goats). The same Theo van Gogh made the movie *Submission*, together with Ayaan Hirsi Ali, a Dutch politician from Somalian Islamic background, very present in the media and very outspoken in accusing Islam of misogyny and tyranny, and an obstacle to human freedom and dignity. *Submission* charges the Islam and the Koran with promoting violence against women. Theo van Gogh was savagely murdered in Amsterdam on 2 November 2004, by Mohammed Bouyeri, a self-proclaimed defender of Islam who left a note on Van Gogh's body explaining mainly why he had *not* murdered Hirsi Ali, although that in a sense for him was apparently the obvious thing to do. In the course of all this, with Hirsi Ali together with other Members of Parliament being secretly moved around to different houses and body guarded around the clock for months, the almost proverbial Dutch tolerance for religious differences has turned into what sometimes seems like blatant Islamophobia, and not seldom hatred of all things religious.

In the first part of this issue of *Concilium,* the question is asked what happened to the Western approach to Islam and Muslims, and why. Theo de Wit presents the developments in the Netherlands and the way it attracted attention internationally. He makes clear that the issue of a politics of tolerance is on the agenda again, after an easy multiculturalism has proved to be an illusion. Marcel Poorthuis analyses and criticizes the image of the Islamic and the Western worlds in the influential book *What Went Wrong?* by the American Islam-scholar Bernard Lewis. Lewis's approach seems exemplary for the current presentation of Islam and its history in the Western world. Marc De Kesel unearths the fundamentalist logic present in the letter Mohammed Bouyeri left on Theo van Gogh's body, making clear that fundamentalism is not so anti-modern as it is usually presented and showing how an obsession with death is at the heart of it. Karin Vintges deals with the way Islam is contrasted with Enlightenment and especially feminism in the self-presentations and the media-presentations of influential female critics of Islam like Ayaan Hirsi Ali in the Netherlands and Chahdor Djavan in France. We should not think about Islam and feminism as alternatives, she argues, but engage in a process of mutual learning with the growing movement of Islamic feminism.

Contrasting a free, peaceful and secularized Western modernity to a tyrannical, violent and religiously backward Islam seriously twists reality. Not only does this mask the violence of Western modernity and its unsettling consequences worldwide, but it also marginalizes the plurality and the intense discussions within Islam. The relations between religion and violence, religion and oppression, religion and politics, religion and democracy, and religion and liberation are debated at least as hotly in the Islamic world as they are in the Christian world. From this debate, Islam has a contribution to make to attempts at shaping the world's future and this contribution deserves to be taken seriously. This is not to deny that there are violent tendencies in the Islamic world – as there are in other religions, that there are groups of Muslims defending discrimination and violence against women and preaching war against modern civilization. But the strange alliance between Islamists and secularists, claiming that *this* is typical for religion in general and an inalienable part of Islam in particular, needs to be challenged.

The second part of this issue of *Concilium* presents new developments within the Islamic tradition that are not commonly known. Nelly van Doorn-Harder presents female and feminist interpretations of the Koran and shows how women use it as a charter for their rights. Asma Afsarudin shows how the Hadith-literature, the Islamic traditions on the words and deeds of the Prophet, is interpreted. Thomas Michel presents the neo-Sufi spirituality of Turkish scholar Fethullah Gülen and his followers as directed to dialogue and ethical responsibility. Erik Borgman introduces the three intellectuals from a Muslim background that were awarded the prestigious Erasmus Prize in 2004 for their humanist contribution to today's culture: Fatema Mernissi, Sadik Al-Azm and Abdulkarim Soroush.

As a journal, *Concilium* is dedicated to the idea that religious traditions are important because they can offer fruitful and liberating visions on the human condition and the world, on what liberation might mean and on how to reach it. An important point of this issue is to show Islam as an important religious tradition in this respect, making clear that Christian theologians should re-enforce the dialogue with it, notwithstanding the current climate and without denying the various problems we are confronted with. The third part opens with Hans Küng, who recently published a highly praised book on Islam, giving his view on the meaning of the Muslim tradition in today's world. Pim Valkenberg discusses in what sense the concept of Judaism, Christianity and Islam as 'Abrahamic religions' still has a future. Erik Borgman defends the idea that Christianity and Islam can help each other to become a space of liberating Enlightenment by keeping on searching for the transcendent and hidden but nevertheless present God they confess.

This issue of *Concilium* closes with a documentary section in which Theodore Gabriel contrasts the way Islam and Muslims are presented in the media to the way Muslims understand themselves, and Lucinda Ory documents reactions from British religious leaders and institutions to the bomb attacks in London.

I. Islam and Enlightenment: New Figurations

The Necessary Disillusionment
The Netherlands after the Murder of
Theo van Gogh

THEO W.A. DE WIT

The Netherlands in turmoil

In recent years foreign commentators have become interested in the small country by the North Sea which has long been known for its ancient and honourable democracy and has a long tradition of groups of different religious and ethnic backgrounds living alongside each other peacefully. They have also begun to take an interest in a nation that had not had a politically motivated assassination for more than five centuries – until during the election campaign in May 2002 Pim Fortuyn, a politician, was shot by a milieu activist and until the cruel murder of the director and film critic Theo van Gogh in November 2004, carried out by a young Muslim who to this day is convinced that it was his religious obligation to do this.

Thus at the end of 2004 the French expert on Islam Olivier Roy in an interview with a Dutch newspaper expressed his astonishment about the rapid development of the debate in the Netherlands with regard to the integration of immigrants and in particular with regard to living alongside Muslims: 'What took us thirty years, you did in five.' The statement of the well known US columnist William Pfaff was more blunt and even harder: in his view politics in the Netherlands had been dominated for far too long by a strange and fatal combination of 'good intentions and illusions'.[1] I think that both were right in their assessment.

There is indeed something strange in the way in which in the Netherlands one initially cherished the ideal of a 'multi-cultural society' in a good-natured or even over-zealous manner, only to – in the last five years – bid it farewell again in heated debates. Outsiders might be left with impressions of superficiality, of instability and of a lack of political confidence. In my country the doubts with regard to 'multi-culturalism', the well-meaning welcoming of cultural identities in the 'multi-coloured Netherlands' were quickly followed by a critical assessment of the 'emptiness' of a culture of tolerance which had been made possible by an un-reflected and un-committed embracing of cultural diversity. Those who merely 'tolerate' others, thus one of the core arguments of this criticism, make no claim to be taken seriously by others. The political debate about the integration of immigrants thus also took on the dimension of a public debate about the 'values' by which tolerance is carried but which also limit it. Already before Theo van Gogh, well known for his aggressive criticism of Islam, was murdered, the public debate concentrated on the freedom of speech and the public engagement with Islam as well as on the 'right' relationship between democratic politics and religion in general.

After this murder a heated debate erupted in the press and on television about terrorism and fundamentalism, about the character and the essence of Islam, a debate which at times could take on the form of a real 'Kulturkampf' between irreconcilable principles. 'Enlightenment' and Humanism were presented as being in contrast to 'Fundamentalism' and even religion in general. And this was not limited to being a mere struggle of words. There was a surge of racist crimes such as arson attacks on Muslim schools and church buildings. We also have to take seriously the consequences of the murder of Theo van Gogh for the political life of the country: politicians and opinion-makers whose lives were threatened and who had to go into hiding, restriction with regard to the formation of political parties, threats of self censorship of artists etc.

It appeared more and more as if the technocratic depoliticization, which had been characterisic of the shape of the commonwealth for the last ten years, was being followed by a culturalization, which is uncharacteristic for this country, presented by some even in a somewhat apocalyptic tone. This country, so the concerns voiced by some commentators, was in danger of becoming a country of rapidly changing sentiments, while in the recent past it had been a country of more or less stable political ideologies. Already prior to the politically motivated murder of the brilliant politician Pim Fortuyn, the country had been captured by a 'pressure cooker' culture, in which emotions and fears were heightened with every incident once it had been registered and intensified by the media. Pim Fortuyn himself had been very skilled in his use of the media. He was able, particularly in appearances on television, in a very short time to challenge and snooker the political establishment. The evident insecurity and embarrassment of the political elite in the face of what was soon to be known as the 'Fortuyn phenomenon', revealed a moral emptiness and a politics in the face of a vacuum of power which was not unrelated to an important but crumbling foundation of the culture of tolerance in the Netherlands. For the line of defence behind which the ruling parties withdrew in the confrontation with the challenges presented by Fortuyn remained weak: this politician was introducing a right-wing intolerance into the Netherlands and was thus violating a general taboo; and not Fortuyn but the ruling coalition had struggled to win the previous war, the world war against racist National Socialism. But contrary to the widely held views (even abroad), Fortuyn was not a racist but a charismatic popularizer.

The rapid development of the debate about integration and about the Netherlands, about which Roy had wondered, can also be described in a different and more rational way. In my country in recent decades there were different political and political-philosophical answers available to the simple and central question as to what the ultimate end of the 'politics of integration' should be (the necessity of which was denied by none of the political movements). At the core of this there are five answers or a combination of these.[2] They also imply an answer to the question about the kind of political unity which one had in mind, also about the 'we' which formed the horizon or which had to be defended.

A first answer was that integration was not a one-sided process, but that Dutch people themselves had to work together with migrants and their children towards a new multi-cultural society. Integration is successful when such a society takes shape. Within such a society the 'right to diversity' is an important basic right which are in polemical contrast to the asymmetrical demand for enculturation and assimilation on the part of the immigrants.

The second answer emphasizes that migrants and immigrants as well as Dutch people have to respect the general human rights. Integration has been successful when everyone in their immediate environment as well as in dealing with people outside of it respects human rights. Here a potentially universalistic and cosmopolitical 'us' is in contrast with forms of (cultural, national or religious) particularism which is not yet in agreement with human rights or refuses such agreement.

A third, more pragmatic answer regards integration as successful when immigrants reach high achievements with regard to education and are successful in finding employment. The 'us' in this case is defined by the Netherlands, here primarily understood as a successful competitive society and as part of the process of economic globalization. The language used here contrasts for example the so-called 'successful allo-chthones' with 'loosers' in school and on the job market.

A fourth answer emphasizes that migrants must become 'more modern'. In this case, integration is regarded as having been successful if they assimilate more and more to secular and 'enlightened' citizens of Western societies. Secular citizens are presented as being in contrast with and as an example for people with 'fundamentalist', traditionally religious, ethnic and tribally defined loyalties.

A fifth and final answer is that migrants must become integrated into Dutch culture. Integration is regarded as successful to the extent in which migrants not merely take note of Dutch culture and national history but also identify with Dutch customs, sensitivities and over-sensitivities. The 'us' is in this case the nation state of the Netherlands with its national culture and its historic heritage.

In Dutch society and politics during the last ten and especially the last five years we could observe a rapid shift from the first answers mentioned here to the ones mentioned last. Of course, most of the practical and political orientations and suggestions offered in the Netherlands are combinations of these answers which I have presented here in their most succinct and polemical form. In this form they encompass in my opinion in their political and philosophical assessment with regard to their practical consequences a combination of useable elements as well as their unrealistic and inhumane aspects. At first however mainly the apparent initially seemingly elastic embrace described in the 'multi-culturalist' first answer gives rise to concern. It is followed by a drastic rejection. In other words: what are the most important 'good intentions and illusions' (Pfaff) corresponding to their political and philosophical dimension which have dominated Dutch political culture and still dominate it? I will attempt to give a brief answer to this question in the next paragraph. These (interdependent) illusions, which one can find in the Netherlands among the large liberal parties and movements left and right to the centre, concern indeed particular conceptions of 'multi-culturalism', the meaning of tolerance and freedom of speech as well as the status of religions with regard to democratic politics and civil rights and obligations. Only a process of disillusionment on this level which in my country has not finished can in my opinion lead the pluralistic democracy in the Netherlands in the right direction. I will thus also conclude with some remarks on the need for a new balance in this democracy.

The failure of 'tolerance-multiculturalism'

In order to gain a clear picture of the theoretical and practical problems of multiculturalism it is useful to be able to distinguish between multicultural-ism in the strong sense and in the weak sense of the word. The philosophical and ethical inconsistencies of a 'strong' multiculturalism have long been known. They have probably been most astutely described by Alain Finkielkraut in 1987 and by Stanley Fish in 1994.[3] I am therefore able to concentrate on the core ideas here. I am a multiculturalist in the strong sense of the word if I am convinced that all cultures in their core deserve the most profound respect, that they are entitled to shape their own identity and to have their own ideas about what is humane. In this case tolerance is the highest principle for me. This tolerance multiculturalism creates a dilemma for me if I am faced with cultures or religions which themselves refuse tolerance, restraint over against others or the inclusion of those who think differently. I can then respectfully accept the intolerance of such cultures or religions. However, in this case, tolerance is no longer my leading principle. I can also reject such intolerance, but then I no longer respect the culture with regard to that very point where the most essential difference lies.

Let us concentrate initially on the first case: I am then prepared on the basis of the right to be different to grant someone else the right to reject precisely this right. Or I am prepared on the basis of a well-meaning (self-) criticism of Euro-centricity to sing the praises of the other's ethno-centricity. This makes me a universalist with regard to that which is mine and a particularist with regard to that which is different or Other. I am thus in the paradoxical situation which Finkielkraut articulates with such eloquence: on the basis of humanism and respect, thus with 'good intentions' I am led to plead for a 'right to submissiveness'.

A second problem with this attitude is that I am left without defence against ethnocentrism within my own culture. For those on the extreme right can adopt the arguments of multiculturalism without a problem and can go without the nowadays problematic racist terminology. Do they defend the right to be different? Let us just listen to Jan-Marie Le Pen and his followers in many European countries: 'Nations cannot be described as equally of higher or lower standing. They are different, and we have to take into account these physical and cultural differences.'[4] While both agree with the underlying principle of such multiculturalism (the right to be 'different') and including a certain romantic understanding of culture ('our forms of expression are of necessity expressions of a particular culture'), the political consequences drawn from this differ in the case of right wing extremists and hospitable multiculturalists. The final conclusion drawn by representatives of such a 'racism without race' is that it would be a tragic error to allow communities of different civilizations alongside each other as collisions between them would be inevitable. One only has to think of slogans such as 'France for the French' and 'one's own people should come first' etc.

What was extraordinary with regard to the situation in the Netherlands was in my view that it was possible for multiculturalism in the strong sense of the word to escape such embarrassing paradoxes for a long time. Here we encounter a central liberal illusion which had been held in our country for a long time: as long as I can assume that cultural differences are by definition nothing other than differences with regard to lifestyle (which is by nature a matter of everyone's own choice and preferences), my own identity will, on the whole, not be affected or violated by other forms of propriety or identity. Then there will no longer be otherness and difference which could disturb me or which I could even notice. One could call this a 'tolerance without contact', the aseptic tolerance of the *vive la différance*!

This is the source of my assumption with regard to the question why the idea of a multicultural society in the sense of a natural harmony could survive in this country for such a long time. This dream could go on through the combination of a liberal utopia and a collective moral obligation. The liberal dream is the dream of a post-political society – nurtured also by the economic affluence in the Netherlands in the 1990s – or even of a world free from profound (cultural or religious) differences between human beings. Thus we can accept these differences altogether as a form of cultural folklore or even welcome them. This is the utopia of a world without otherness and ultimately also without collective boundaries. Connected with this is a particular understanding of the freedom of speech. The latter is no longer understood in the classical post-liberal-democratic tradition as the vehicle of public debate about the common good but it is the expression of particular identity as chosen by individuals or groups. In a post-political society 'words' are essentially no longer potentially dangerous as they have become socially and politically meaningless.

The collective moral obligation is a matter of faithfully holding on to antiracist discourse, a legacy of the traumas of the Second World War and anti-semitism. Thus doubting multiculturalism is in the Netherlands regarded as tantamount to discrimination and xenophobia.

In the second case in which I highlight the limitations of tolerance I have to surrender multiculturalism in the sense described above. Then I can only be at the most a multiculturalist in the weak sense of the word, a *boutique multiculturalist*, to use Stanley Fish's words. A substantial amount of the disillusionment which has taken place in the Netherlands with regard to being a 'multicultural society' has to do with the increasing awareness of many multiculturalists that in truth they have remained multiculturalists in the weak sense of the word. In the Netherlands, a *boutique multiculturalist* is someone who goes from one multicultural event to the next, who is jealous with envy about the gracefulness of people from the Antilles or the Capverdes, who values cultural differences as long as they can be regarded as secondary with regard to a general identity which all of us human being share. For such lovers of culture, culture is largely something which has something of the (exotic) other. They can accept that there are those who wear a headscarf as a peculiar form of behaviour. They will however start to shiver with regard to the *nicaab*, a form of veil which covers the entire face which some Muslim women have begun to wear in recent years as well as with regard to certain other cultural or religious practices such as female circumcision, ritual slaughtering, honour killings, forced marriages etc. What is admired by such people is the general human *ability* to make their own decisions, not however the actual decisions themselves which are incarnate in concrete traditions or religions. The latter are possibly even an obstacle to the autonomy of the individual. Furthermore cultural decisions cannot stop others or cannot be imposed on others for example through the 'rights of groups' or by the state. Such decisions are precisely as is religion not a corporate concern but merely a private matter. Multiculturalism in the weak sense of the word is at its heart by no means genuine multiculturalism but soon turns out to be a form of universalistic liberalism which has shaken off the reservations and naïvités of multiculturalism in the weak sense of the word.

In recent years in the Netherlands one could see largely the dark side of such liberalism, and in fact always where it went along with a rationalistic ideology of progress according to which humanity is unstoppably on its way to a form of humanistic scientific atheism. According to the opinion of the liberalist disguised as a multiculturalist, those who still want to retain a form of collective but particular identity are wrong with regard to the right form of hierarchy: they prefer the particular to the universal, difference to equality. They must be perceived as an 'in-fans', as a child yet unable to speak for itself which still has to be raised; or even as a fundamentalist who is to be opposed for absolutizing such matters as part of religion. Thus in the Netherlands immediately after the assassination of van Gogh an atmosphere developed in which a liberal avantgarde which proclaimed universal reason was able to judge Islam as such. It is not a coincidence that this polemical atmosphere also generated the term 'fundamentalism of the enlightenment'.

In the way which I have outlined here multiculturalism in the strong sense of the word (which already deemed to be living in the post political idyll of a multicultural society of harmonious and unthreatening identities) changed into a form of militant liberalism which sometimes even chooses to sacrifice its classical liberal legacy (such as democratic tolerance and the freedom of conscience) on the altar of secular authoritarianism which was more reminiscent of a Jacobite revolutionary tradition. Thus I assume that the necessary process of disillusionment in the Netherlands has not yet advanced far enough as neither the folkloric ideal of a *living apart together*, of a mosaic of cultural identities, not the neo-colonial tone with regard to cultural and religious minorities take us any further.

Identity and openness

In order to understand why the public discussion in the Netherlands in recent years has concentrated more and more on 'national identity' and on the place of the religions in this country, we must first of all take into account an economic fact which has become visible all over Europe. Since the second half of the nineteenth century the European nation states have their democratic legitimacy in their ability to represent within the confines of a certain territory and a shared national history social and societal powers and then also to intervene – 'as welfare states' – in society. To the extent in which this was successful it became possible to equate citizenship, nationality and democratic sovereignty. While however democratic political sovereignty is more and more interfered with by economic globalization and the loss of political sovereignty, national cultures at the same time through the development of a trans-cultural space appear to be more and more provincial, contestable, in short contingent civil religions. This experience of the contingency of the liberal and in some ways even libertarian model of Dutch society is by a large number of migrants experienced as by no means evident and thus unwillingly 'profaned'.[5] It is this experience which has thrown the Netherlands into confusion and is an explanation of much of the contemporary *Kulturkampf*. For this experience makes us aware that an open society like that of the Netherlands is vulnerable and the proverbial tolerance of this country is tied to special conditions and should by no means be taken for granted. The fact that with van Gogh's assassination the worldwide phenomenon of religion and terrorism has come to light in our own country has of course given further rise to this awareness of contingency. In the same way as vulnerable and anxious human beings are inclined to shut themselves off, this is also true with regard to angst-ridden states. This is the root of the popularity of populist politicians. The well-known Dutch historian Geert Maak recently described such politicians polemically as 'dealers in fear'.[6] A long time ago the literary sociologist Leo Löwenthal spoke in the same sense of the 'reverse psychoanalysis' of populists.[7] As a good psychoanalyst teaches her patients to live with their fears and neuroses and thus to regain their autonomy, the populist aims to increase the fear and thus to tie his audience to himself and to increase his own political capital.

I want however to make a plea for not diminishing the significance of such populist tendencies and nationalistic voices of protest against the political elite. For to the extent to which politicians present international developments such as migration, economic globalization and European union along with all their socio-cultural consequences as an inevitable and uncontrollable fate, protest against it can conceal a genuine impulse to democratic autonomy. The self-reflection in the Netherlands today and the search for an identity of one's own can also be an effort to find a new balance between tradition and liberty, between dialogue with one's ancestors (J.B. Metz's concept of 'anamnetic solidarity') and personal autonomy, in short between gratitude for the given and the contemporary calling to live together in pluralistic society that will last.

Characteristic for the current confusion in the Netherlands is finally also the ambivalence with regard to religious diversity. While some, not infrequently out of fear of an 'Islamization of culture' (Pim Fortuyn), want to push religion (even further) into the sphere of the private, there are others who plead precisely for this reason for a more visible presence of religion in public life as a contribution to 'social cohesion' or even for a new form of civil religion.[8] Religion understood in the right way however will not allow itself to be confined nor to be made a political instrument. What we can however expect of religion from a democratic point of view is that they as world views or 'comprehensive doctines' (Rawls) surrender their claim to shape society as a whole. This acceptance of the difference between its truth claims and their practical realization in legislation is what democracy calls *tolerance*.

Translated by Natalie K. Watson on the basis of the
German translation by Ansgar Ahlbrecht

Notes

1. William Pfaff, 'Europe pays the price for its cultural naïvité' *The International Herald Tribune*, 25 November 2004.

2. The last four of these are *grosso modo* also named by Siep Stuurman: 'Godsdienst is niet per se anti-modern' NRC-Handelsblad, 7 October 2003.

3. Alain Finkielkraut, *La défaite de la pensée*, Paris, 1987; Stanley Fish, 'Boutique Multiculturalism' in *The Trouble with Principle* ed. Stanley Fish, London, 1999, pp. 56–72 (1. edition 1994).

4. On this experience of (unintended) 'profanization' in a multicultural society see Rudi Visker, *Vreemd gaan en vremd blijven. Filosophie van de multiculturaliteit*, Amsterdam, 2005.

5. On this experience of (unwilling) 'profanation' in a multicultural society cf. Rudi Visker, *Vreemd gaan in en vreemd bliven. Filosophie van de multiculturaliteit*, Amsterdam, 2005.

6. Geert Maak, *Gedoemd to kwetsbaarheid*, Amsterdam/ Antwerpen, 2005.

7. On the phenomenon of populism in Europe see *Populismus in Europa*, Zeitdokument 4, 2002. There also (p.11) the reference to Löwenthal.

8. On the different positions with regard to this point see e.g. *Religie als bron can sociale cohesie in de democratische rechtsstaat. Godsdienst, overheid en civiele religie in een post-geseculariseerde samenleving* ed. B.C. Labuschagne, Nijmegen, 2004.

What Went Wrong with Bernard Lewis? The Uncertain Debate about Islam and the Enlightenment

MARCEL POORTHUIS

I. The rhetoric of the European debate on Islam and the Enlightenment

As soon as the question about Islam and the Enlightenment arises in Europe one gets the impression that the questions grow more rapidly than the answers. On hearing the word Enlightenment few think of rarely known facts such as the fact that from the tenth century Baghdad was an important centre of philosophical and religious exchange. Jews, Christians and Muslims studied each other's scriptures, and even the followers of Zarathustra and the Manichees were included in the debate. These debates were at times heated and their outcome by no means always peaceful, but out of them emerges a remarkable knowledge of the tradition of the others. If we even go as far as thinking of the influence of philosophy as a means to support one's own religious persuasion with arguments of reason and not merely with proof texts from scripture, one can clearly speak of a religiously enlightened 'humanism'. As is well known, one can find a similar picture of an intellectual inter-religious culture a few centuries later in Spain. Even if we take into account that the 'Golden Century' at close inspection was much less brilliant than is widely assumed, even then an exchange between religions in the light of reason was possible. Such enlightened forms of exchange are primarily to be credited to the world of the East which had a shared language, Arabic, and which made a shared philosophy, through the filter of Arabic, i.e. Platonism and the philosophy of Aristotle, available to all.[1]

Even if these forms of enlightened religious thought are very important and even if their non-European origin must be thought about, the question if Islam needs an Enlightenment means something else. In such discussions historic dates frequently disappear into the background. This is a discussion which in current debates appears in rather surprising contexts. Some prominent examples: the Belgian cardinal Godfriend Danneels argued that Islam needed a 'French Revolution' as the Roman Catholic Church had in his opinion experienced it.[2] This position is somewhat surprising. Until today the Roman Catholic Church's attitude towards the achievements of the French Revolution cannot be described as altogether positive: along with the demand for 'liberté, égalité, fraternité' went the full frontal attack against religion. The result was the radical separation of church and state in France, the infamous 'laicité'. However, precisely the extent and the limits of that radical separation are under discussion today, as religion seems to have been banned into the realm of the private and that influence of religion on politics is branded as not permissible. The neutrality of 'laicité' thus appears to be used as an ideological tool against religion, and the emphasis on tolerance paradoxically takes on traits of intolerance. The discussion about the wearing of headscarves seems to be the peak of this tension between tolerance and intolerance. By the way, not only Islam and Roman Catholicism seem to struggle with the French Revolution, even the emancipation of Judaism from the French Revolution onwards appears to have two sides to it: on the one hand liberation and equality, on the other hand restriction and reduction of Judaism to being a private confession at the expense of those ethical aspects which are characteristic of Judaism, of a particular language, a particular ritual and a particular country.

The separation between religion and politics is not to be confused with the separation between church and state. On the contrary: a strong democracy is able to mobilize precisely the multi-coloured contribution of religions and world views. Cardinal Danneels obviously wants to draw the attention of Islam to the significance of the separation between religion and state and thus uses the 'French Revolution' as a code. The ambiguous significance of the 'French Revolution' for religions up to this day thus is left in the dark. It is clear that the Cardinal's point of view initially raises more questions than answers. By the way, Turkey, currently applying for membership in the European Union, under Atatürk's leadership modelled itself very clearly on the western separation between church and state.

Something similar can be said about the views of Cardinal Ratzinger, now Pope Benedict XVI, with regard to his plea for a Europe which is conscious of its religious roots. This ardent plea quite rightly points to an intellectual oblivion of ethical and religious traditions in favour of a not very thought through relativism. The latter not only puts its own values last, but also has no real regard for other convictions and truth claims[3] At the same time Ratzinger's plea also raises a large number of questions which for the time being remain unanswered. Ratzinger speaks of a 'Judaeo-Christian tradition' which is supposed to be the foundation of European norms and values. This 'Judaeo-Christian tradition' is even used as an argument against Turkey's joining of the European Union. But was the conjunction of Jews and Christians really such an immoveable foundation for Europe? Would it not be appropriate at this point to point out that Europe has persistently denied the Jewish roots of its history, with the murder of six million Jews as its sad low point? How is one then able to use the Judaeo-Christian as an argument, even as a buffer against Islam in Turkey? In addition, the question arises if we should not speak more of the conjunction between Judaism, Christianity *and* Islam. This is done for example in the significant Roman Catholic document *Nostra Aetate* (1965) which speaks of Abraham as the father of the *three* faiths.

These examples of the view that Islam is in need of an Enlightenment indicate that what is required on our part is a thorough self investigation as well as correct knowledge of Islam. This not only applies to Christians, who voice their opinions in this regard, but also to those who start from a post-Christian point of view. The debate about European norms and values which are supposed to serve as a buffer against Islam will in the long run not succeed in defining the values under question, let alone to delineate them from what is taught within Islam. With regard to my own country I see a twofold perspective with regard to views on Islam. First of all the Churches, which argue for a good relationship and who – with the exception of conservative Protestant and Evangelical movements – identify a religious connection between Christians, Jews and Muslims. In addition, there is also the post-Christian perspective, represented by philosophers of culture, who frequently brand the monotheistic religions as sources of intolerance and violence and who perceive Christianity and Judaism to be at best domesticated forms thereof. In the context of the latter arguments one does not shy away from speaking about Islam in an essentialist way and from blaming it for its supposed *essential* tendency towards violence and intolerance. Thereby in my opinion Muslims in the Netherlands as marginalized in a very dangerous way. Such arguments without a doubt intend to oppose extremist forms of Islam but instead favour the social isolation of Islam in Europe. If one wants to gain Muslims as allies against religious extremism and terrorism, a plea quite rightly voiced by some in the Netherlands, then one would have to make them feel in the first place that they are entirely accepted and have the right to live out their religion in complete freedom. The call for an Enlightenment of Islam in the Netherlands has generated an patronizing and intolerant atmosphere which Muslims cannot experience as an invitation to a shared covenant.

Even the internationally renowned film *Submission* by the Somali politician Hirsi Ali and the director Theo van Gogh who was murdered by a Muslim extremist indicates an essential connection between the Koran and the beating of women if a text from the Koran is projected on to the bare skin of a woman.

Thus already talking about Islamic terrorism instead of Al Qaida terrorism is a subconscious classification of Islam as a whole as religion which is by nature prone to violence. Furthermore, expressions like 'the problem of Islam' or 'What went wrong with Islam?' suggest a mono-causal explanation for a very diverse range of problems originating from very disparate geographical and cultural contexts which are often not very well kept apart. On the level of rhetoric this can be compared with the way in which people in the first half of the twentieth century spoke about the 'Jewish question' or the 'Jewish problem' when one should rather have spoken of the 'non-Jewish problem'. Perhaps such arguments conceal a kind of inner insecurity with regard to the norms and values of Europe viz. the Enlightenment which is held up as a condition for Islam. While the Enlightenment can also be understood as a call for tolerance over against other religions viz. as a critique of certain forms of ethno- and Euro-centrism, here it is held up in a very Euro-centric way as a demand for Islam. An apt example for this insecurity with regard to the actual content of the values and norms of Europe was recently offered by the Dutch minister for administrative renewal and royal matters, Alexander Pechtold. On 3 September 2005 he argued in the newspaper *Trouw* against the demonization of Islam in the Dutch media. In the same breath he added that Muslims had been coming to live in the Netherlands since the Middle Ages and that they were 'not used to nudity and certainly not to our Dutch sperm shows'.

The minister's words indicate an original and perhaps not even entirely untrue view of European values and norms which in any case is clearly distinct from the churches' views mentioned above! To put it more generally: European norms and values are for the latter obviously judgements as to what is good and evil which are not shared by all. Thus a generally *shared* culture does in spite of Danneels and Ratzinger not actually exist, and this absence is almost characteristic for Europe. Instead there are 'open', i.e. not clearly defined and filled values: freedom of speech, tolerance, liberty. Through the confrontation with Islam Europe is reminded of the meaning of these values as well as – in an embarrassing way – also of its limits.

II. Bernard Lewis: What went wrong?

The role of experts on Islam in the debate as to whether Islam is in need of an Enlightenment is significant. Some point to the brilliant achievements of Islam (such as myself in the introduction to this article), voice warnings about categorical judgments and pretend more or less to be allies of Muslims in Europe. They are frequently accused of ignoring the difficulties which Islam has with modernity in favor of politically correct reflections on particular periods in the history of Islam or particular interpretations of the Qur'an which are insignificant in today's Islam. Other Islam experts table all manner of historical data with the intention of showing that today's problems with Islam and modernity are by no means coincidental but rather are deeply rooted and inherent in Islam itself. The best known and most outspoken representative of the latter group is probably the North American scholar Bernard Lewis. His impressive academic achievements make his statements about Islam very prestigious, so that they can be very influential with regard to public opinion and even US-politics. In the rest of this article I want to show that this prestige is not justified. A careful reading of Bernard Lewis' book *What went wrong?* (2004)[4] reveals that most of his statements on Islam are based on rhetorical exaggerations and unauthorized conclusions from arbitrarily selected data. This leaves the reputation of Lewis' scholarship and profound expertise on Islam untouched. I myself am not able to compete with this, and furthermore I am more of an expert with regard to Judaism and early Christianity. In my opinion it is not so much his knowledge of particular historical facts but the questions which went wrong in Lewis' case. The questions asked by him are frequently too complex, and frequently too quick a connection is made between historical facts and the present. The remaining gaps are all too easily filled with private opinions not under discussion and with political and cultural observations of his own making. However this is to anticipate the conclusion of this article.

The title *What went wrong?* insinuates the same as the essentialist views outlined above. Thus there is to be *one* Islamic problem with *one* cause which is to be found in the Islamic world. How does Lewis do this? He begins with an indeed knowledgeable overview of the history of the wars between Islam and the West. He shows how Islam was during the first centuries of its existence indeed successful on the battlefield, but had to withdraw during the later centuries: western technology overtook the Arabic countries. The facts listed are no doubt correct. They are however interpreted in a rather strange way as if its military backwardness is part of the Islamic problem. It would however be equally logical to think that the *progress* of the West, from the Cold War to nuclear weapons is part of the problem! The same applies to Lewis' view of culture. The Arabic world has to its own detriment smugly neglected Western culture. By way of proof Lewis reminds us of the fact that in 1929 a rather remarkable map was found in Istanbul, a Turkish version of Columbus' map of the New World. 'Unknown and hitherto unseen', so Lewis. However, by the same logic one could argue: the Turkish civilization has preserved a map of the world which has been lost in the West, perhaps through ignorance or neglect. Furthermore, a sixteenth-century Turkish book on flora and fauna of the New World 'remained unknown until it was printed in Istanbul in 1729', so Lewis. Here too the negative conclusion is that it is the Arabic world which is not interested in Western society, drawn from Lewis' point of view. Is it not rather remarkable that there was already in the sixteenth century a Turkish book about the New World which in 1729 was even printed?

In conclusion Lewis argues that the Western world had made huge efforts to learn the languages of the orient while this was not the case the other way round. This is indeed true, and the scholarly achievements of Oriental Studies are impressive. Meanwhile sufficient evidence has been found as to how much these studies were connected with colonial rule. Whichever way we look at matters, America and Western Europe were not colonized by Islam in the same way. Here Lewis once again admits himself that during the nineteenth century many Arabic students went to the West in order to immerse themselves in Western languages and Western technology.

The book's basic thesis *What went wrong?*, i.e. that Islam was not able to keep up with the developments of the last two centuries in the West, deserves to be looked at more closely and must at the same time be subject to careful critical analysis. Is it true that Arabic countries could not keep up with Western music or have they just tried to maintain their own musical tradition and their own musical idiom? If Western music is then also presented as a product of co-operation and team spirit which is supposed to be simply lacking in the Middle East, then this is plain obscurantism. Characteristic for the Western classical music from the nineteenth century onwards is the romantic lonely genius, an image which has even pro-foundly influenced our image of the composers of the eighteenth century (Beethoven!).

Furthermore, some have compared the symphony orchestra with a dictatorship, a comparison which is as bizarre as Lewis', although in the opposite direction. Lewis does not compare the 'enormous backwardness' of the Orient with regard to classical music with the no doubt equally enormous backwardness of the West with regard to oriental musical forms and techniques. Lewis notes an interest in pop music in the Arabic world, but ignores the growing influence of 'exotic' styles of music on pop music (such as Rai). His argument only makes sense if one assumes that European music is the norm for the whole world.

In contrast a real, actual difference between East and West is the development of early capitalism in the West. Lewis however ignores the numerous theories which seek to explain the development of capitalism in the West, such as those of Tawney and Weber, to name but the best known. It is not impossible that the understanding of economy, work ethic and askesis and thus also the accumulation of gain, possibly based on a particular form of Protestantism, may be able to offer an explanation for the different developments in Europe and the Middle East. With regard to the largely secularized European society a purely religious explanation is far too one-sided. The enormous economic growth in Far Eastern Asia, connected with a certain ageing process in Europe, let alone the recent *economic miracle* in China cannot be explained in this way. Even more complicated is the question whether the value of a culture must be measured by its economic growth. The difference between the cultured thoughtful Greeks who developed no technology and the pragmatic Romans who were great architects is well known.

For Lewis certain cultures are superior to others, sometimes due to their military superiority, sometimes due to their economic expansion. These are however dubious and obviously contradictory criteria. Elsewhere Lewis accuses Islam of its supposed militant character! Even oil is relativized away by Lewis with the statement that oil will soon be replaced by another source of energy! Here I dare say that for the time being the USA are still very interested in oil.

Here the West itself appears to be embroiled in a rather difficult debate: where is it supposed to find the value and the identity of its own culture, its own norms and values, if just their ancient foundation, religion, is on the way back? In the end of the day egalitarian western societies ultimately favor progress more than Islamic countries where equality was preached initially, but where Jews and Christians had always had a subordinate status. But was it not a European society, and not an Arabic country, where so many Jews were murdered?

The abolition of slavery is supposed to be a further factor in which the West had shown its superiority. However, was this not as difficult in the West as in the East where slaves had always been treated better? Here too Lewis gets entangled in contradictions. In the past the slave trade was without a doubt for the West a basis and thus also a proof for its economic superiority – we have only to think of the Golden Century of the Netherlands. But should now its abolition be proof of superiority?

What must be called into question most critically is the tacit assumption that the collision of the cultures has caused a 'problem'? Lewis does not look at the most obvious cause of the entire problem of the *clash* between the West and the Arabic countries, including the precarious situation of America in Iraq. This is in my opinion the loss of the Soviet Union in the balance of deterrence which, threatening though it may have been, guaranteed a certain stability in the Middle East. America would not have invaded Iraq if Russia had still been as strong as it was 25 years ago. One does not have to be on the extreme left to see that it was the economic relationship between America and Saudi Arabia – which is by the way the actual breeding ground for terrorists – which prevented military action in that country. Therefore it was not a 'clash of civilizations' which triggered the unrest in the Middle East, but economic interests and the lack of a balance of military power. The cultural backwardness of the Arabic world in contrast to the more 'superior' West thus appears in a somewhat different light. More than likely Lewis's starting point, his construct of competing cultures, is already dubious and bound to fail.

The question regarding the integration of Muslims in the Netherlands which is often raised in the same breath with the aforementioned political issues, has very little to do with the situation on a world-wide level. Lewis' reflections therefore contribute nothing to the solution of the tensions outlined above, such as we also know these for example in the Netherlands. On the contrary: his essentialist views with regard to Islam rather work in the direction of a marginalization and isolation of Muslims in Europe, as they make the degradation of Islam intellectually and socially acceptable.

Wouldn't Dutch people struggle just as much to integrate and be integrated into any (non-Western) culture as Muslims do here, provided they do not segregate themselves off into cultural enclaves, as is often the case today?

Lewis is unable to look beyond his own Euro-centric perspective, and the way in which he interprets his data does not contribute to a solution but is rather part of the problem. Like Danneels and Ratzinger, Lewis too neglects to undertake an analysis of Islam alongside a thorough self-reflection on Western culture and those values on which it is supposedly or actually not founded. Thus their diagnoses diverge as much as they do: while the cardinals see Christianity as a constituent element of Europe, even if in Danneels' case in the purified form of the separation of Church and state, for Lewis it is not Christianity itself but this very separation which is the positive element of the West.

Lewis has a number of excellent books to show for himself, and yet the weakness of his book *What went wrong?* can be explained very easily. Especially where Lewis goes beyond the boundaries of his area of expertise, the history of Islam historical analysis degenerates into a regurgitation of his own personal political convictions and to a rather populist view of culture. His so-called comparison of cultures constantly leads him to inconsistencies, to contradicting himself and to a selective handling of data. Perhaps, so I would like to say, playing on a variation of Lessing, only the kind of culture which manages truly to respect another can be regarded as highly cultured. And this every culture, be it Islamic or western, should take to heart. If Christianity does not wish to lose its credibility, it must not allow that which it has to show for itself as valuable for Europe to be used against Islam.

Translated by Natalie K. Watson based on the
German translation by Ansgar Ahlbrecht.

Notes

1. Cf. M. Poorthuis, B. Roggema and P. Valkenberg, *The Three Rings. Textual Studies in the Historical Trialogue of Judaism, Christianity and Islam*, Louvain, 2005.

2. G. Danneels, *The role of ethics in an enlarged Europe*, unpublished lecture, 23 September 2004,. Cf. a similar text by Danneels in *Europa werkelijkheid en opgave. Verkenningen in het spoor van Guardini* ed. by S. Waanders with G. Danneels, O. von der Gablentz et al., Damon Budel, 2004.

3. J. Ratzinger, 'Über den Selbsthaß Europas', *Avenire* 14 May 2004.

4. B. Lewis, *What went wrong? Western impact and Middle Eastern Response*, Oxford 2002.

The Right Use of Death
The Fundamentalist Logic in Mohammed Bouyeri's *Open Letter to Hirsi Ali*

MARC DE KESEL

In the evening of 2 November 2004 Mohammed Bouyeri assassinated the director Theo van Gogh in Amsterdam. It was a conscious deed. This is obvious from the letters alone which one was supposed to find on his dead body (for he himself had expected to be shot by the police), and from the open letter to Hirsi Ali which he left on the body of his victim. In a tedious way the latter outlines the motives, not so much why he 'executed' van Gogh, but rather why he did *not* do this to Hirsi Ali, even if it was her whom he wanted to get at with van Gogh's assassination.

It is worth the effort to read this second letter carefully. It shows how Bouyeri's fundamentalist discourse revolves around a heightened sensitivity which is by no means alien to modern thinking. This is a heightened sensitivity with regard to death, and more precisely, dealing with death, the use one can make of it. This is, as I will show, one of the elements which show how modern fundamentalist discourse is, even, and especially in those places where it is directed most strongly against modern thought.

The right to diversity

The letter is addressed to Ayaan Hirsi Ali, an allochtone of Islamic origin, a member of the second chamber of the Dutch parliament and for Bouyeri an 'infidel fundamentalist' unlike hardly any other. Using her he attacks all Western modern thinking 'infidel fundamentalists'. This is more evident from the tone which he uses than from his actual arguments. Of the latter, the letters have few, if any. Thus the author insinuates that these are already 'known'.

This by the way they are. We are dealing with the usual range of critical accusations raised by Muslim fundamentalists of the great Islamic critics of the twentieth century such as Sayyid Qutb[1] and Ali Shari[2] – to name but two: the West is decadent with regard to its morals, promiscuous in its sexual morality, apostate with regard to its religion, imperialist with regard to politics. Bouyeri does not repeat any of this in his attack on Hirsi Ali. He does not regard the evil which she has committed as her personal 'fault'. The regretful state in which Muslims find themselves is first and foremost their own fault.[3] And be it only because they have lost their ability to put up a fight. And that they have lost because they like Christians have become unfaithful to their God. Thus they have become apostate to that which they are themselves: i.e. Muslims, a community – an 'Ummah' – which is joined together around the one God by reading aloud from the unique book of the unique prophet. The Muslims of today, despised and humiliated as they are, only receive what they deserve, thus Mohammed Bouyeri.

It is from this self critical position that Bouyeri thinks he can attack Hirsi Ali. As a member of the Second Chamber of Parliament she had at some point suggested that 'Muslims should when applying for jobs be tested with regard to their ideology'. Now it is her turn to test her own political clique, thus uttered Bouyeri. In it are even Jews, so he claims, and thus she is steeped in an ideology which is at least as evil as that of which Muslims are accused.[4] He subsequently quotes from the Talmud, e.g. that 'only Jews are human beings', that 'non-Jewish women are called animals' or that 'even the best of the *gojim* (non-Jews) must be killed'. Now treat your Jewish friends in the same way as you treat us Muslims, and forbid them to continue to teach from the Talmud. But, so he closes for the time being: for that you are just too 'weak'.

Here Mohammed Bouyeri deals primarily with himself, with his own identity and with how in a world of liberty and equality he can retain this identity with its own particular characteristics. For it is this which, so he feels, our modern society does not permit him. He is unable to be *different* from the others; he is unable to be *himself*. And if he is misjudged in this, then at least he wants others to be misjudged in this too, as the reason for this can be found in them too. In short, so Bouyeri against Hirsi Ali, if you humiliate Muslims on the basis of what their Koran says, then you must humiliate your Jewish party friends on the basis of just those same things which can also be found in their Talmud.

Here Mohammed Bouyeri is closer to modern thinking than he would like to be, so much is he caught up in a typically modern problem. He wants the recognition as 'equal' for an identity which is not easily 'identical' or 'equal' to everyone. In his way he articulates less the problem of true Islam, than the problem of modern political identity and its relationship with that which it makes possible: the fact that in politics all people in their diversity are equal.

The Death and the sentence

Mohammed Bouyeri in his Open Letter goes on to rage against another one of Hirsi Ali's political proposals. She had, so Bouyeri, voiced the idea that young Muslim children should be explicitly invited to choose between Islam and modern culture, between 'their creator and the constitution'. It is first and foremost for you to realize that you have been presented with the choice, replies Bouyeri and then goes on to add: 'You, Ms Hirsi Ali, are given this opportunity to inscribe this your right once and for all on the pages of the book.' Not the right which she is proclaiming here and now, so it becomes clear, but the 'true' right. She could once again inscribe – engrave – herself on one of the pages of God's book which in a world of moodiness and sin offers a clear separation between truth and lies.

What is the truth which she is asked to 'engrave' in the book? 'Death', is the answer. Mohammed Bouyeri's entire letter revolves around death. Death as the only certainty we have in life. But also death as the certainty, *of which we can make use*, with which we can write, inscribe ourselves for example in the book, which keeps a record of all certainty and truth. Mohammed Bouyeri's letter offers a touching invocation of death as the only certainty left to us human beings:

> There is one certainty in the whole of existence; and that is that every-thing comes to an end. A child born unto this world and fills this universe with its presence in the form of its first life's cries, shall ultimately leave this world with its death cry. A blade of grass sticking up its head from the dark earth and being caressed by the sunlight and fed by the descending rain, shall ultimately whither and turn to dust. Death, Miss Hirsi Ali, is the common theme of all that exists. You, me and the rest of creation can not disconnect from this truth.

The tone of these words is religious and pompous, but we can also read this incantation as a touch of the typical modern sentiment in the face of our mortality. No-one can claim ownership of the absolute truth, for no-one can escape from our mortality.

These realizing sentences however are immediately followed by a long entreating invocation of the 'day of judgment', 'sentencing day':

> There shall be a Day where one soul can not help another soul. A Day with terrible tortures and torments. a Day where the injust shall force from their longues horrible screams. Screams, Miss Hirsi Ali, that will cause shivers to roll down one's spine; that will make hairs stand up from heads. People will be seen drunk with fear while they are not drunk. FEAR shall fill the atmosphere on that Great Day:

Let your spontaneous fear speak, thus Mohammed Bouyeri, addressing Hirsi Ali directly, wants to say; for that will teach you that everything and all are subject to the judgment of a judging God, a God who has been good enough to reveal himself and his judgment and that is a revelation which the Ummah of Muslim brothers and sisters hold in high regard and you should do the same before it is too late.

Bouyeri does not mention that this judgment has already been carried out with regard to Theo van Gogh. The presence of van Gogh's dead body makes such a reference obsolete. Bouyeri, according to his own statement, has only carried out the judgment which van Gogh has himself brought upon himself by insulting Allah's prophet and thus Allah himself. It was just inevitable that tormented Muslims who for so long had to put up with the insults of infidel 'aggressors', who finally act. And this act only confirmed the 'death' in which van Gogh had been straying for years. For what else could his pretence of a life, apostate and cut off from the living God, be called? Already years ago he incurred 'eternal damnation', and the deed that had been carried out on him was only the 'right use of death' in order to make him and all people see the judgment. But you infidels will not be able to understand this at all, so Bouyeri accuses at once.[5]

And yet he is convinced that Hirsi Ali is not devoid of all hope. The mere fact that he had killed not her but Theo van Gogh is an indication of this. There is another chance for her, so Bouyeri: if she too *makes right use of death*. This is the exit to safety which he has in store for her. His entire *drama of cruelty* was aimed at just that:

If you really believe this, then the following challenge should be no problem for you. I challenge you with this letter to prove you are right. You don't have to do much: Miss Hirsi Ali: WISH for DEATH if you are really convinced you are right.

This is the centre piece of Bouyeri's letter and it betrays how modern thinking and religious revisionism are intertwined here. It ought not to be 'an imposition on you', so he entreats Hirsi Ali, to wish for her own death. For her there is no God, no ultimate meaning of life. For her death is merely death: this is the ultimate misreading of the message of Islam, the final form of apostasy. And yet this is not entirely incompatible with what the Prophet had intended for people of your kind, so he indicates using a reference from the Qur'an:

Say: "If the ultimate abode with God in the hereafter is exclusively for you, not for others of mankind, then you must desire death if you are truthful." But they will never desire it because of what their hands have committed before. Verily, God well knows the unjust. (Qur'an 2.94,95)

To make the right use of death: for Mohammed Bouyeri this is the only thing that is left for Hirsi Ali to do. She herself can carry out the judgment which the divine will pronounce over her and which faithful disciples of his prophets should normally carry out on her. This death sentence, carried out on herself, will make it possible for her to be saved at the last minute from the hands of the unbelievers.

She may then have carried out her own execution, as for her death as well as life are meaningless; and yet her deed is nonetheless an ode to the meaning of life warranted by God and a service to the *Ummah*, the world-wide fellowship of believing Muslims. It is an act of true martyrdom, a way finally to 'inscribe herself' on the pages of the book of life, created by Allah. This act by the way will make her equal to Bouyeri, for he himself will *make right use of death* and will also 'desire death'.[6] In vain, so it seems: for he himself was not ripped apart by bullets as he had hoped.

For it is this 'right use of death' alone which warrants the certainty of overcoming and allows for this 'burning struggle to be different from all that have gone before it'. 'No discussion, no demonstrations, no parades, no petitions; merely DEATH shall separate the Truth from the LIE.', he goes on to write. Bouyeri rejects all modern discursive methods with which we present our problems in public and where we want to offer a place to Islam within our pluralistic, multicultural society. There are false ways to get to the truth. The only way is that of 'DEATH'. It is precisely this which unbelievers want to avoid, he goes on to say: they ignore the judging power of death.[7]

Desiring death as ignoring death

'Demise', dying', 'death': this is the great theme in Bouyeri's discourse. It gives him a sense for modern thinking where reference to finality and death moves everything into the relativizing light of day. For Bouyeri and other Muslim fundamentalists this is the cause for the crisis of modernity. For death is the only absolute Lord left for us. This means that all other Lords, even God, are dead. It is therefore no surprise, according to their interpretation, that the modern West has gone so far astray – with regard to religion, economy, military power, sexuality and morals.

According to Bouyeri's Muslim fundamentalist logic we modern Western people make a *wrong* use of death. To put it more precisely: we make *no* use of death at all, we regard death as something of which no-one, not even God himself, *can* make any use. And it is precisely this which is the reason why we have become so apostate without measure. For it is not death which is the Lord over life and death but God, so our own religion used to teach us once upon a time, and so we ought now to learn from Islam, as we have allowed our own religion to wither. Therefore it is the holy obligation of Muslim fundamentalists not merely to preach the faith, but to sow it even with terror – i.e. with the fear of death. The fear of death alone can restore to modern rootless humanity a sense for the judging power of death. You western people ignore this and try therefore to ignore death, so Bouyeri closes his discourse; and he points out to 'America', 'Europe', 'the Netherlands' and 'Hirsi Ali', 'the unbelieving fundamentalist' that they will 'go under' And, so he goes on to say immediately, repeating himself: 'I know this for certain.'

Is he really that certain that he will not along with his certainty 'go under' himself? Here is the core as well as the weakest link of the entire argument, and here the paranoid character of his fundamentalist logic is brought to bear. Death which he himself uses to make others aware of it by pointing out to them – 'as you know for certain' – that they will go under, does not apply to himself. Not that he does not know that he will go under himself. On the contrary: he anticipates it by taking the bull by the horns and 'desires death';

for it is this which has been given to Muslims, even an apostate Muslim like Hirsi Ali, by the grace of God. But this anticipation of death is nevertheless a harsh *misjudgment* of death. It equates it with the One who lives beyond death. His death is an exchange to eternity, a warrant that after the last judgment – the judgment, the ultimate separation between life and death – he will sit at the table of the living.

The fundamentalist obsession with death is therefore primarily a strategy to deny the reality of death. And this of course at the same time makes one blind for reality. In their eyes the latter is so marred by sin and moral corruption, that it in itself can be regarded as death. Once one has understood this, one will be aware that one no longer lives in this reality but already in a world which will arise from the ashes of sinful reality. The existing world must be destroyed. To serve the world therefore comes to mean: to destroy it. The same applies to the fellowship of believers. The *Ummah* from which fundamentalists live is not the actual existing fellowship of Muslims but the *Ummah* of which they dream, which will exist once all unbelievers, even all 'weak', moderate and (hence) degenerate Muslims have been purged out of it.

Such a form of behavior which is characteristic for fundamentalism can also be at the heart of a struggle *against* fundamentalism. To the extent in which the struggle follows the logic of war, this risk increases. The longer this obtains the more the enemy will have to be used to project ones own deficits on to them and then to deny them. This 'perverse' danger is a threat to the contemporary global 'war on terror' which the current US President seeks to organize.

Religion to which death and finality are central is not immune from this form of behavior. Mohammed Bouyeri's Open Letter is an example of the way in which Islamic logic can fall prey to this. However, even Christian logic as such is not resistant to this evil. On the contrary: death is central to Christianity as it is to no other religion, and its teaching on resurrection and eternal life can also result in a misjudgment of death and finality. As soon as one speaks in the same breath of this misjudged death, as soon as one presumes to speak in the name of God and to deem oneself to be an interpreter of his judgment, this misjudgment is in danger of taking on the perverse form which we have seen in the case of Bouyeri.

Religion is always also a culturally constructed way in which this danger can be carried out, in Islam as well as in Christianity. In the form of monotheism it pays homage to the conviction that no-one can claim to be

God, because God alone is God. This is the critical side of Monotheism –
even a form of Religionskritik Instead of being lulled into the security that
our God is God as such, monotheism demands a constantly critical attitude
which time and time again seeks to exorcise this firm certainty. If one is per-
mitted to speak the name of God, then only to say that no-one can speak in
this name just like that, not even in the moment when one says it. However,
the case does not rest for monotheistic culture with such a paradox: this
paradox is a reminder of the lasting desire of human beings to speak in the
name of God and to be united with the fullness of God, and the point here is
neither to destroy this desire (which is impossible), nor to allow it to exist
uncritically, but to 'bring it into culture', to cultivate it as something with
which we will never come to terms and *fortunately* never come to terms, if
only because such terms would destroy our desire. And, to say with Jacques
Laçan: we *are* desire, unresolved, unquenchable desire.

Translated by Natalie K. Watson based on the
German translation by Ansgar Ahlbrecht.

Notes

1. Sayyid Qutb (1906–1966), initially poet and literary critic. Became the great
ideologist of the Egyptian Muslim Brotherhood and was thus sentenced to death in
1966. John Gray (in *AlQaeda and What it Means to Be Modern*, London, 2003) points
to an almost straight line which links Qutb with Bin Laden in the sense that the
latter studied at the King-Abdul-Aziz University of Jedda studied with Sayyid's
brother, Muhammed Qutb.

2. Ali Shari'ati (1933–1977) is one of the initiators of the revolution in Iran. Like
Qutb he lived for some time in the West (e.g. in Paris). Amongst others he translated
Che Guevara and Frantz Fanon.

3. 'The fact that you can openly spew your hatred is not to blame on you, but on
the Islamic Ummah. They have ceased their task of resistance against injustice and
is sleeping it off.' This quotation and all other quotations from Mohammed
Bouyeri's *Open Letter to Hirsi Ali* are taken from http://www.balder.org/articles/
Theo-van-Gogh-Murder-Open-Letter-To-Hirsi-Ali.php. Quotations which are
not marked otherwise are from this text.

4. 'Your proposal is very interesting, more so because the application of it
unveils the rotten faces of your political masters (when they would of course be
tested honestly and they would openly reveal their ideology). It is a fact that Dutch
politics is dominated by many Jews who are a product of the Talmud schools; that
includes your political party-members.'

5. 'You, as unbelieving fundamentalist, of course do not believe that a Supreme being controls the entire universe. You do not believe that your heart, with which you cast away truth, has to ask permission from the Supreme being for every beat. You do not believe that your tongue with which you deny the Guidance from the Supreme being is subject to his Laws. You do not believe that life and death has been given you by this Supreme being.'

6. 'To prevent that I were to be accused of the same, I shall wish this wish FOR you: My Lord, give us death to make up happy with martyrdom. Allahoemma Amien.'

7. Here he refers to chapter 62 verse 8 of the Qur'an: 'Say: 'The death from which you flee will surely meet, then you shall be returned to the Knower of the unseen and the seen, then he will inform you of whatever you used to do.' (this and other quotations from the Qur'an: *The Koran. Translation* Translated by S.V. Mir Ahmed Ail, New York, 2004).

Some Hypes and Some Hope:
Women and Islam in the Western Media

KAREN VINTGES

In September 2005 Ayaan Hirsi Ali, a Dutch politician of Somali descent, was invited by the board of the University of Amsterdam to deliver a speech on the occasion of the opening of the academic year. In her speech, Hirsi Ali argued that Islamic religion does not allow for any curiosity and therefore it is incompatible with science. She appealed to the students of the University to do research on how Islamic culture and religion play a major role in the backwardness of the Islamic world, and she accused the staff of the University of Amsterdam of being 'politically correct' for avoiding this question. In a debate in the University's weekly, following this speech, those who protested against the University's policy to invite Hirsi Ali along with the critics of her speech were denounced as being 'cheap', 'dangerously suggestive' and 'immoral'.

Tradition versus modernity

The tone of this debate is illustrative of today's polarized climate in the Netherlands where the issue of women and Islam plays a significant role. Especially since September 11 attacks, not only in the Netherlands but throughout the Western world, there has been a polarization, around the question of whether Islam can be reconciled with modernity. Modernity in these controversies is often defined as the amalgam of progress through science and reason, democracy, individualism, the emancipation of women and secularism. It is seen as western in origin. In contrast, the Islamic world emerges as backward, because it is seen as firmly entrenched in a religious tradition. 'Modernity versus tradition' is the framework of this debate on Islam which is at the heart of contemporary political discourses on the social organization of society.

Large portions of the Dutch population today are convinced that Islamic culture and religion are extremely hostile to women. Not only in the Netherlands but throughout Europe women's oppression by Islam has become a critical topic, for instance in Belgium and particularly in France. Many people in France (feminists included) believe that Muslim women and girls should be rescued by law and prevented from wearing the head-scarf, which the French see as a symbol of oppression per se. The issue of women in Islam has become prominent in these countries through the interventions of a few women who have left Islam and are 'hyped' in the media. In the Netherlands Hirsi Ali in articles and lectures and interviews repeatedly argues that Islam is 'backward' for its inherent oppression of women. She is critical of the left and claims that 'on the one hand they support ideals of equality and emancipation, but in this case [the condition of women in Muslim communities] they do nothing about it; they even facilitate the oppression'. She calls this the 'paradox of the left.'[1]

Hirsi Ali has risen to a prominent role in Dutch public life not least through the support of some influential feminist politicians and opinion leaders. Meanwhile however there are others, including many feminists, who are suspicious that the outspoken concerns about the oppression of Islamic women may in fact be an excuse to attack and suppress Muslims rather than a genuine concern. During the last decades many third world women have accused western feminism of imposing its own standards on women at a global level. For this reason many feminists in the past years have practiced a withholding gesture towards women from other cultural backgrounds, asking themselves how to reconcile a feminist view which wants to end any oppression of women, with a multiculturalist approach of respect for other cultures. Throughout her work Hirsi Ali attacks this withholding gesture as well as the multiculturalist approach. She has published two books, *De zoontjesfabriek* [The Factory of little Sons] and *De maagdenkooi* [The Cage of Virgins].[2] To understand her position more fully we have to take stock of her explicit reference in one of her books to the influential feminist philosopher Suzan Moller Okin in *De zoontjesfabriek*.

Liberal fundamentals

Okin wrote a famous essay, entitled 'Is multiculturalism bad for women?' (1999), and an earlier article in which she complained that the global movement for women's rights in the past years had missed the intellectual and political support from almost all western feminists, 'who were bending over backward out of respect for cultural diversity'.[3] According to Okin liberalism should be the universal norm of a global feminism. She attacks the multiculturalist point of view that minority cultures should be protected by special rights. The cultural practices that are at stake deal for a large part with the personal, familial and reproductive side of life, for this reason the defence of cultural practices is likely to have much greater impact on the lives of women and girls than on those of men and boys. Many of these cultural practices in the domestic or private sphere violate the rights of women. Establishing group rights to enable minority cultures to preserve themselves is therefore 'bad for women'. Polygamy, forced marriage, female genital mutilation, punishing women for being raped and unequal vulnerability to violence, are practices and conditions that are not unusual in many parts of the world, while the norm of gender equality at least formally is endorsed by Western liberal states, so Okin argues. It would be better for women if certain cultures became 'extinct' or preferably were encouraged to alter themselves, rather than preserved. Only those minority cultures should be fostered by the state that respect liberalism's 'fundamentals'.

In line with Okin's position, Hirsi Ali argues for a prohibition of Islamic schools, and for active intervention by the state to prevent female circumcision and honour killings. Clearly inspired by Okin's appeal to liberalism's 'fundamentals', she in 2003 made a move from the Social-Democratic to the Liberal party, for which she became a member of parliament. Since then she has been omnipresent in the media. In the summer of 2004 she caused a real media-hype herself by launching a film on Dutch television entitled *Submission I*. In this short film, texts from the Qu'ran are shown on naked bodies of women who have been physically abused. When its director Theo van Gogh was murdered by a Muslim extremist in the autumn of 2004, he claimed that Hirsi Ali was to be the next. She went into hiding and, returning in public after a few months, announced that she would not remain silent and would continue to speak up for Islamic women. Hirsi Ali since then has had special housing and is safeguarded around the clock. This year she was placed on *Time Magazine*'s list of the hundred most influential people in the world today. Her message in the media fairly represents the views she presents in her books, interviews and speeches in parliament, where she argues that Islam is backward and inherently oppressive to women, the latter being the reason why she is compelled to speak up on behalf of Islamic women.

In France the very same role which Hirsi Ali plays in the Netherlands has

been allocated to the French-Iranian writer Chahdortt Djavann, author of
the famous booklet *Bas les voiles!* [Down the veils!, 2003].[4] Djavann was
compelled to wear the veil in Iran after the Iranian Revolution for ten years
until she fled from her country. In her book she expresses her anger about
this, comparing the veil with the yellow star the Jews were forced to wear by
the Nazis. Like Hirsi Ali Djavann attacks the approach which sees immigrants as members of distinct communities on religions or ethnic basis which
should be respected. 'God knows what kind of common identity this should
be and of which the veil should be one of the symbols!' In her recent booklet
Que pense Allah de l'Europe [What Allah thinks of Europe, 2004] Djavann
warns against an Islamist 'take over' of Europe.[5]

Like Hirsi Ali in the Netherlands, Djavann was supported by some
influential feminists, such as Elisabeth Badinter, a self-confessed great
admirer of Simone de Beauvoir. Badinter devoted a chapter of her recent
book *Fausse route* to the issue of the veil, which she like Djavann considers a
symbol of women's oppression per se.[6] Both Djavann and Hirsi Ali argue
that all Muslim women and girls are victims of an oppressive religion and
culture and that Western secularism is the only road to emancipation. Both
are embraced by influential opinion leaders and are depicted in the media as
feminist heroines who have had the courage to stand up against women's
oppression in Islam. Their articles and interviews are published throughout
the most important national newspapers and both are invited to lecture in all
the public forums in their countries. Hirsi Ali and Djavann thus play a
prominent role in the ongoing debate in the West on Islam, framed in terms
of modernity versus tradition.

Another 'media-voice' in this debate is Irshad Manji, a Canadian journal-
ist who represents herself as a lesbian and a Muslim believer. Although
Manji is often mentioned in the same breath with Djavann and Hirsi Ali, for
instance on websites from right wing extremists, such as that of the Belgian
'Vlaams blok' and a Dutch website called 'Dutchdisease', she herself refuses
to take sides against Islam as such. In her book *The Trouble with Islam,* she
appeals to Muslims to practice 'Ijtihad', the Muslim tradition of independent thinking which flowered in the Islamic golden age between 700 and
1200 C.E.[7] In contrast to secularist positions, Manji does not abandon her
Muslim identity, but asks for reinterpretations of the Qu'ran and for a
change of the Islamic tradition from within. In her case the media attention
given to her often does not correspond to her own message. She is often one
dimensionally represented in the European press as an Islam critic *pur sang*

in connection to the issue of Islam and women, and therefore can hardly appeal to the Muslim women and girls who she would like to reach.

Islamic feminism

Throughout Europe many Muslim women and girls mainly feel insulted by the repeated message that all Muslim women and girls are victims of an oppressive religion and culture. In the Netherlands many of them are appalled by Hirsi Ali's campaign and close themselves off from what they experience as an overall attack on their identity. They often insist that 'not the Qu'ran but men' are the real problem and they search for an approach to the issue of Islam and women that can reconcile Islam and feminism instead of emphasizing its irreconcilability.

In contrast to a strongly secularist feminism, during the last decade we find an new approach to the issue of Islam and feminism which can take into account these voices of Muslim women and girls as well as Hirsi Ali's and Manji's feminist concerns. Since the 1990s new perspectives and new practices are developing which demonstrate that Islam and gender justice are not inherently incompatible. They refer to the dynamic and diverse history of Islam, for their reinterpretations of the Qu'ran and Islamic historical traditions. They highlight the egalitarian spirit of Islam's ethical spiritual message, and the active role of women in the history of Islam. Other studies show the active role of women in Islamic societies today, demonstrating that Islamic women are by far not the passive, oppressed creatures that many Western feminists hold them to be.

In her classic *Women and Gender in Islam* Leila Ahmed focuses on the ethical spiritual side of Islam. She goes into the dynamic and diverse history of Islamic religion, articulating its ambiguity with respect to the role of women.[8] Whereas the Qu'ran explicitly states that men and women are equal in the eyes of God, Muslim women are often oppressed by Islamic moral codes, especially in the form of family law (the Sharia). Ahmed argues that the ethical-spiritual side of Islam can be elaborated into a feminist perspective, that – as she states in the last lines of her conclusion – does 'enable women to pursue without impediment the full development of their capacities and to contribute to their societies in all domains'. Ahmed's book has offered the vocabulary and tools for Islamic women to create themselves as Islamic feminists, transforming the tradition of Islam by way of reforms internal to their culture.

In her *Qu'ran and Woman* Amina Wadud has also emphasized the egalitarian spirit of the Quran.[9] According to her, the Qu'ran again and again has to be interpreted in new contexts. Wadud herself reinterprets the text with the modern woman in mind, demonstrating how the key principles of the text can be adapted to a constantly changing world. There are some limitations that exist in the text itself but they are a reflection of the seventh century Arab world, the context in which the Qu'ran was revealed. The key assumptions of the text, and its overall world-view are egalitarian, and in the Qu'ran there is an emphasis on gradual reform. Wadud's work has met an enthusiastic response of women from Muslim countries as is indicated by Wadud herself in the preface to the US edition of her book. Both Ahmed's and Wadud's studies have inspired Islamic women to fight for gender justice within Islamic culture and religion, and to transform entrenched positions. In an article entitled 'The Quest for Gender Justice: Emerging Feminist Voices in Islam' Ziba Mir-Hosseini states that 'by the late 1980s, there were clear signs of the emergence of . . . . a gender discourse that is 'feminist' in its aspiration and demands, yet is "Islamic" in its language and sources of legitimacy'.[10] She concludes that 'there is a theoretical concord between the egalitarian spirit of Islam and the feminist quest for justice and a just world'. In some Muslim countries, there are now Muslim women organisations which have a feminist agenda (like for instance Malaysia's 'Sisters in Islam'). In regard to this new emerging discourse of Islamic feminism, we can ask ourselves whether and how it transforms feminism in turn. Do these new perspectives of Islam and gender justice involve a critique of, and an alternative to, current feminist positions? Should feminists perhaps revise their concepts of freedom and 'enlarge their mentality'?

In a recent study on the Egyptian Women's Mosque Movement, *The Politics of Piety*, Saba Mahmood, in line with earlier critiques of third world women, criticizes Western feminism for imposing a Western normative framework in which individual freedom and autonomy are the key assumptions.[11] Mahmood pointedly argues that autonomy and self-realisation are two different things. The ideal of individual self-realisation is to be found in every culture. The typical Western combination of autonomy and self-realization is too limited a view on what human flourishing can be. Mahmood does away with the concept of freedom all together, and therefore, as she argues herself, with feminism.

In my view however instead of dismissing feminism as such, we should direct our criticism at strongly secularist feminism that equates freedom with the autonomous, separated self. Free individual self-realization in the sense of free ethical-spiritual self-creation (in opposition to religious fundamentalism which merely demands obedience) is a value which is to be found in many cultures and religions. Feminism has to revise its concept of freedom so as to include ethical spiritual self-creation within the context of religion. Freedom should be re-conceptualized in terms of the lives people make for themselves *within* meaningful communities and traditions, opposing domination in these traditions through a modern attitude of 'working on the limits'.[12]

Since the beginning of the last century, feminism has been an integral part of the discourse of 'modernity versus tradition'. In *Women and Gender in Islam* Leila Ahmed reports on how feminism was imported in Egypt by Western colonizers. In Iran feminism was in its inception launched by secular parties in opposition to the Islamic tradition. Currently in Morocco and Iran, as well as in Egypt and Malaysia, a discourse of Islamic feminism is developing which challenges the debate on Islam in terms of modernity versus tradition, by showing modernity within religion.

Mutual learning

Western intellectuals are only just beginning to realize that mutual learning is at stake in cross-cultural dialogues. In my opinion it is the ethical-spiritual dimension that is so much alive in religious contexts that can inspire Western culture to rethink its own past and find some new answers to its future. The new discourse of Islamic feminism which is gradually emerging is unfortunately not very well known in the Western world. However, there is some hope for change. A conference on Islamic feminism in Amsterdam in May 2005 was well publicized in the media, mainly because of the presence of Amina Wadud who made a furore some months before due to her leading a mixed-gender prayer service in New York, an event which was reported widely in the international media.

There was a large feminist conference in Amsterdam in September 2005 where women from all cultures gathered. They discussed how they could cooperate, and the way they did this parochialized the discourse of the 'clash of cultures' between Islam and the West. This conference was reported very positively in the media. New perspectives thus are emerging for coalitions between religious and secular feminists. Whilst these coalitions already exist in Muslim countries like Iran and Morocco, the hypes around strongly secular feminists in the Western media make it difficult for these coalitions to arise in the Western world. It is about time that the voices of Islamic feminists here are also heard.

Notes

1. In an interview in the *Guardian*, 17 May 2005.

2. Ayaan Hirsi Ali, *De zoontjesfabriek: Over vrouwen, islam en integratie*, Amsterdam, Augustinus, 2002; *De maagdenkooi*, Amsterdam, Augustinus, 2004.

3. Suzan Moller Okin, 'Feminism, Women's Human Rights and Cultural Differences', *Hypatia* 13 (1989), no.2, 32–35; Suzan Moller Okin and respondents, *Is Multiculturalism Bad for Women*, ed. J. Cohen, M. Howard and M.C. Nussbaum, Princeton, Princeton University Press, 1999.

4. Chahdortt Djavann, *Bas des voiles!* Paris, Gallimard, 2003

5. Chahdortt Djavann, *Que pense Allah de l'Europe*, Paris, Gallimard, 2004.

6. Elisabeth Badinter, *Fausse route: Reflexions des 30 années de féminisme*, Paris, Odile Jacob, 2003.

7. Ishad Manji, *The Trouble with Islam: A Wake-Up Call for Honesty and Change*, Toronto, Random House, 2003.

8. Leila Ahmed, *Women and Gender in Islam: Historical Roots of a Modern Debate*, New Haven, Yale University Press, 1992.

9. Amina Wadid, *Qu'ran and Women: Rereasing the Sacred Text form a Woman's Perspective*, New York:, Oxford University Press, 1999 (first edition Kuala Lumpur, Penerbit Fajar Bakati, 1992).

10. Ziba Mir-Hosseini, 'The Quest for Gender Justice: Emerging Feminist Voices in Islam.' *Islam 21* 36 (2004), p. 3.

11. Saba Mahmood, *Politics of Piety: The Islamic Revival and the Feminist Subject*, Princeton, Princeton University Press, 2005.

12. See my article 'Endorsing Practices of Freedom: Feminism in a Global Perspective', in *Feminism and the Final Foucault*, ed. D. Taylor and K. Vintges, Urbana and Chicago, University of Illinois Press, 2004, 275–299.

II. Enlightened Islam? – New Developments

Women Reading the Qur'an

NELLY VAN DOORN-HARDER

During the last week of October 2005 an International Congress on Islamic Feminism was held in Barcelona.[1] This congress had some remarkable aspects that show a breakthrough in the role Muslim women play in the Qur'anic sciences. Those speaking at the congress represented Muslim women scholars and activists from a variety of countries who all were striving to improve the position of women within Islam based on teachings of the Qur'an. For them, the Qur'an is the direct word of God that guarantees women rights and securities that were taken away from them in the centuries following the death of the Prophet Muhammad. While male interpreters corrupted the texts that in principle are egalitarian, influences from local cultures added to the misogynistic points of view that developed over time. In the view of these women scholars and activists, theological assumptions have given rise to sexual inequality that can only be corrected by re-reading the Qur'an from a women's point of view.[2]

This contribution traces how women have started to take hold of the Qur'anic text themselves. They do this as individuals such as Riffat Hasan and Asma Barlas who originate from Pakistan, or with male collaborators such as Zainah Anwar from the Malaysian Sisters in Islam (SIS) movement, and Lily Zakiyah Munir from the Indonesian project called CePDeS that aims at raising the awareness of students in the *pesantren* (Qur'an schools) about women's rights and human rights. No longer leaving the important work of interpreting the holy texts to men, these women and men are slowly changing Muslim attitudes and mindsets about women. This particular exercise not only expresses itself in scholarly activities, but also is being translated into activism for women's rights and developmental work.

The growth of this trend can be attributed to the reality that women all over the world now have educational opportunities that were closed to them in earlier times. Even the venerable Al-Azhar University in Cairo now allows women students with the result that its women's department for

Islamic and Arabic studies has a female dean, Dr. Souad Saleh. Further-more, Muslim countries such as Malaysia and Indonesia are fast moderniz-ing and industrializing. According to Zainah Anwar, Executive Director of the Malaysian Sisters in Islam organization, women in such countries 'will no longer accept their inferior status, not even when it is justified in the name of religion. Today's women will not accept that Islam actually pro-motes injustice and ill-treatment of half the human race.'[3]

Islamic feminism?

The trend that women are taking hold of the Qur'anic scholarship also has led to what is loosely called 'Islamic feminism'. The term 'feminism', how-ever, does not mean that these women see the world through the same prism as western feminists. Western ideas of liberal feminism are perceived to lead to individualism and selfishness.[4] Especially, the idea of the 'autonomous and self-reliant individual' does not correspond to the ideological frame of these Muslim feminists as they consider the good of the community to overrule their individual wishes. These women are feminists in the sense that they want to liberate women from the shackles of religious and cultural injunctions and that they seek religious, social, economic and political equal-ity with men. Yet their goals and even beliefs are not monolithic and some of the women involved in this movement hold ultra-conservative positions.

What connects these women, whether conservative or progressive in thinking, is that they are deeply committed to Islam. Their point of refer-ence is the Qur'anic message that according to their reading brings 'mercy for all creatures' (Q. 21.107), and frees 'human beings from any oppression and discrimination due to sex, race and ethnicity' (Q. 49.13). They consider their religion as one of the strongest weapons in the fight to improve women's conditions since in their interpretation it preaches justice for all and equality between men and women (Q. 33.35).[5]

The Qur'an

Concerning the rights and status of women, the Qur'an presents a double message. Several verses stress equality, especially concerning religious observance (Q. 33.35). Based on their religious observances, both men and women can claim paradise (Q. 40.8). The Qur'an also teaches that women and men were both created from the same spirit (*nafs*) (Q 4.1, 6.98, 7.189).

And it states that both Eve and Adam were tempted by Satan (7.20–22), meaning that it does not put the burden of the original sin on Eve. In fact, the Qur'an does not recognize original sin at all. Furthermore, it refers to husband and wife as 'each others garments' (Q. 2.187) and it recognizes a woman's burdens related to childbirth (Q. 46.15). It even provides instructions concerning breastfeeding the child and the age of weaning (Q. 2.233). In principle, it provides women with certain rights within the marriage and allows them to manage their financial means independently from the husband.

However, these egalitarian texts are paired with texts such as those in Q. 4.34 that customarily have been interpreted as assigning to men the right to beat their wives in cases of disloyalty, disobedience, or ill conduct. Male-oriented interpretation of this verse has led to severe domestic violence. In the same verse we find the phrase that 'men are in charge of / or the protectors of (*qaww,m°n*) women because God has given the one more than the other, and because they support them from their means'. The debates around this verse have only just begun and are mostly interpreted as a reference to man's superiority over women. Feminist interpretations however have started to question the traditional meanings of the word *qaww,m°n* and have provided alternative meanings such as that it points at the fact that men should provide for their wives while these take care of the children. Qur'anic verses that traditionally have been interpreted from a male-biased point of view are also reflected in popular traditions – ascribed to the Prophet – such as those stating that the majority of those entering hell are women, and that a woman has only half the brain power of a man's.

Reformist interpretations

The process of rethinking the roles and rights of women in Islam began at the end of the nineteenth century in several places within the Muslim world. Ensuing movements called for the abolishment of veiling, segregation and polygyny and demanded education for girls. The Egyptian scholar of Islam Muhammad 'Abduh (1849–1905) pushed the debates forward by calling for an independent investigation of the religious sources; a method called *ijtihad*. Furthermore he proposed to bypass the teachings of the four legal schools, the *madhhabs*, and the results of the subsequent *fiqh* (jurisprudence) science that he considered to be a body too cumbersome to lead to change.

Abduh's new hermeneutical method was called 'reformist' or 'modernist' and became an alternative to the methods of the traditionalist scholars who applied the teachings of the jurisprudence. Jurisprudence teachings were heavily influenced by customs and ideas from the local cultures that were prevalent in the Middle East during the formative years of Islam. During the first centuries of Islam, local interpreters must have rejected certain texts while ascribing authority to others. Studies such as Brannon Wheeler's *Applying the Canon in Islam* have pointed out that in this process it was not always the text that mattered, but the authority assigned to it by the transmitters of the religious and legal system.

Wheeler for example has observed how the early interpreters of Islam manipulated the traditional interpretations in order to establish certain forms of authority.[6] As the tradition thus emerging was transmitted through pedagogical means, the canonical authority of certain texts became fixed.[7] Especially where the role of women in Islam is concerned, this has led to instances where Muslim scholars bypassed Qur'anic injunctions that are egalitarian towards men and women, giving preference instead to texts that led to denigrating the status and morality of women.

With many Muslim countries witnessing trends of Islamist or more extremist interpretations of Islam, the preference for texts denigrating the status of women seems to have increased. As Zainah Anwar observed: 'Be it in the area of fundamental liberties of women's rights, the tendency displayed by the [extremist] religious authorities is often to codify the most conservative opinion into law.'[8]

Women reading the Qur'an

Reading the Qur'an from a woman's point of view thus should have a double agenda: firstly to focus on the egalitarian texts of the Qur'an and its related sources such as the *Hadith* (tradition), and secondly, to weed out teachings that have entered Islam via the *fiqh* and other sources that were shaped by local cultures; thus the *fiqh* has to be re-interpreted as well.

The first exercise is the one most current and practiced by scholars such as Fatima Mernissi, Riffat Hassan, Asma Barlas, and Amina Wadud. They reside mostly in western countries where they enjoy freedom of expression. The second exercise is practiced less widely as it requires deep knowledge of the Islamic law and jurisprudence. So far one can find examples of men and women trying to cleanse the Islamic jurisprudence from centuries of cultural overgrowth in Iran, in Indonesia, and to a certain extent in Malaysia.[9]

One of the goals of these exercises of analyzing the Islamic frames of thinking and the resulting rules, is to change the injunctions as they are codified in the law; especially the Muslim family law. This law is based on Islamic law, and in principle it is meant to improve the status of Muslim women but often contains injunctions that are considered restrictive to a woman's rights to divorce, custody of children and her movements outside the house. Several Muslim countries have introduced changes in the legal code that protect a woman's position by raising the minimum age for marriage, and guaranteeing women stronger rights in the case of divorce. Legal changes however still comply with local cultures and the demands of their respective religious establishment, with as a result that the regulations of the personal code remain central in the gender debates and in re-reading the Qur'an.

Fatima Mernissi

Moroccan Fatima Mernissi and Riffat Hassan from Pakistan are among the first two scholars who tried to understand why the Islamic sources became misogynistic. In her dissertation *The Veil and the Male Elite followed by Women and Islam: A Historical and Theological Enquiry.*[10] Mernissi investigated how the Qur'an and *Hadith* were influenced by patriarchal discourses that reduced women to secondary citizens. In order to understand how religious teachings have been manipulated, she used sociological analysis and, while being careful not to oppose the sacred texts, she has laid bare the inner workings of Muslim societies as based on those texts.

Mernissi has paid close attention to trends of Islamism that since the 1980s have promoted texts by misogynist scholars from the thirteenth through nineteenth century. These texts led to a growing obsession with women's bodies and social roles and have led some Islamists to promote practices such as polygyny and child marriage.[11] Speaking about female sexuality, her conclusion was that most feared is disorder or chaos (*fitna*) when women's sexual power would prevail in society.[12] This fear has led to segregation, veiling and limitations and a woman's freedom. According to Mernissi, it has developed into the reality that '[t]he entire Muslim social structure can be seen as an attack on, and a defense against, the disruptive power of female sexuality'.[13]

Fatima Mernissi's work has been seminal to Muslim gender discourses. Her work has inspired many women and men to re-read the Qur'anic sources and perhaps the greatest victory for Moroccan women has been the recent revision of the *Mudawwanah*, the Moroccan Personal Status Law. These reforms were instigated by King Muhammad VI who wished to pave the way for Moroccan women to participate in all sectors of the national life. For example, the practice of polygyny has been limited considerably, only allowing a man to take a second wife if he provides proof of sufficient economic means to take care of two households while the marriage has to have the official consent of his first wife and a judge. To justify the far-reaching changes introduced into the Moroccan law, the king referred to his right to exercise *ijtihad*.

Riffat Hassan

Riffat Hassan's work has scrutinized the controversies surrounding the *Hadith* literature and the influence it had on the views on women. She has focused especially on the development of the idea that woman was created from Adam's rib and thus is born with an intrinsic crookedness.[14] She found that these teachings and those blaming Eve for the Fall were taken from the creation story in Genesis 2.18–24 and its elaborations in the Jewish Tradition since the Qur'an does not provide them. In spite of this reality Riffat observed that 'many Muslim commentators have ascribed the primary responsibility for man's Fall to woman'.[15]

Her research into the Traditions and related literature, has led Hassan to focus her studies on the religious human rights in the Qur'an. This exercise has led to the following conclusion:

> I believe that the Qur'an is the Magna Carta of human rights and that a large part of its concern is to free human beings from the bondage of traditionalism, authoritarianism (religious, political, economic, or any other), tribalism, racism, sexism, slavery or anything else that prohibits or inhibits human beings from actualizing the Qur'anic version of human destiny embodied in the classic proclamation: "Towards Allah is thy limit". (Q. 53.42)[16]

Both the works of Fatima Mernissi and Riffat Hassan testify of the reality that the quest to find justice in the Qur'an operates from various ideologies. Women and men involved in these activities find their inspiration in a variety of sources that range from the United Nations' Universal Declaration of

Human Rights, to Islamic jurisprudence (*fiqh*). The movement is becoming wide-ranging and not only addresses women's issues but also, for example, those concerned with poverty, suppression, democratic rights, children's rights and human rights.

Re-reading the *fiqh*

Unlike the male interpreters going before them, many women scholars are moved by personal experience. Fatima Mernissi observed the lack of women's freedom when growing up in a harem, while Riffat Hassan's life work changed when Pakistani women suffering under newly introduced laws curtailing their freedoms (the so-called *hudud* laws) asked her to join their cause. Indonesian women who studied in the Qur'an schools (*pesantren*) faced similar experiences when they realized what the traditional *fiqh* texts taught at those schools said about women.

One of these texts was the *Kitab 'Uqud Al-Lujjain fi Bayan Huquq Al-Zaujain (Kitab `Uqud)* (Notes on the mutual responsibilities concerning the clarification of the rights of spouses) by Imam Nawawi (Muhammad Ibn Umar al-Bantani al-Jawy, 1813–1898), written around 1874. It was a text that according to the respected religious leader Bisri Mustofa, 'went to a man's head' (*membuat lelaki besar kepala*).[17] Concerning a wife's duty, the text states for example:

> A wife should always feel timid when in the presence of her husband, obey his order, be silent when he speaks, stand up to greet him when he comes and goes, adorn herself at bedtime by using perfumes and washing her mouth, always wear make up in the husband's presence, but leave it off when he is not around, not harm his honor or possessions when he is not at home, respect his family and friends, when he brings home a meager income still consider this as big, never reject his advances even while sitting on the back of a camel, not fast or go out without his permission. When she trespasses any of the rules mentioned, the angels will curse her until she becomes aware [of her bad behavior], [she has to obey these rules] even when her husband is abusive.[18]

The text was based on the Islamic injunctions that were current in Mecca where Shaykh al-Nawawi wrote it in the nineteenth century in order to teach his two wives who both worked and earned the family's income.

In the majority of Muslim countries, the greatest challenge facing women is their lack of religious expertise. Since the 1970s, Indonesian women connected to the Nahdlatul Ulama organization that represents over forty million Indonesian Muslims, have gained this expertise in the *pesantren*. Thus they became well equipped to join men in the exercise of interpreting the Qur'an and its related texts. After identifying the text of the *Kitab `Uqud* as the most detrimental to the frame of reference concerning women formed in the *pesantren*, a team of women and men started to re-edit the text with references to the Qur'anic texts about women, showing how their interpretation could have become so misogynistic.[19] The newly annotated edition of the text has been distributed to *pesantren* all over Indonesia and forms an attempt to change the mindset of generations to come.

Worldwide waves

The repercussions of women reading the Qur'an are world-wide. In some countries they are more noticeable than in others but women are slowly gaining the education required to interpret the Qur'an and there is no way back. In this newly developing landscape we witness women pushing the boundaries of the male religious authority. Especially now Muslim communities have settled in Western countries, more women have access to education, and can benefit from freedom of speech and equal opportunities guaranteed by the states. No longer do authoritative expressions of Islam come from the heartlands in the Middle East only. Abdennur Prado, Secretary of the Catalonian Islamic Board expressed this sentiment in the introduction he wrote for the International Congress on Islamic Feminism that was held in Barcelona, September 2005:

> In the context of modern societies, where the weight of the media is so great, it is necessary to make room for pluralistic expressions of Islam. Establishing a different view point breaks with the monolithic belief that the fundamentalists seek to introduce. It is important to offer alternatives, to make room for discussion and to facilitate the breaking of patriarchal and unilateral models.[20]

The activity of women breaking the mould of male authority happens in a variety of expressions. The US-born African American Muslim scholar Amina Wadud created a tornado of Muslim criticism and comments when she led the Friday prayers for men and women on 18 March 2005. Some were quick to remark that neither the Qur'an or *Hadith* have an injunction against women leading men and women in prayer, and that if a woman has the knowledge required to deliver the Friday sermon, she can do so.

Islamonline reacted with a fatwa by the conservative religious leader Yusuf Qaradawi who stated that this was an act unheard of throughout Muslim history. The gist of his argument referred to a woman's body 'whose physique naturally arouses instincts in men'. None of the counter arguments were based on the Qur'an.[21]

The waves of change however need not to be so high and Muslim women follow a great variety of approaches to interpret the Islamic injunctions. Returning to Al-Azhar University Dean Dr Souad Saleh, while being a career woman who is a prominent public speaker on Islamic issues, according to her, the essence of a Muslim woman's duty is 'to be a conscientious mother and home-maker. The Muslim man is the head of the family and the bread-winner. If a woman feels that she can honestly combine a career with her first obligation as a mother and home-maker, then so be it.'[22]

Notes

1. See http://www.feminismeislamic.org/eng/

2. Part of the material discussed in this article can be found in my forthcoming book, *Women Shaping Islam. Indonesian Muslim Women Reading the Qur'an*, University of Illinois Press, forthcoming 2006, and in the article 'Gender and Islam' published in the revised *Encyclopedia of Religion*.

3. Zainah Anwar, 'Gender Issues. New Directions of Islamic Thought and Practice: Exploring Issues of Equality and Plurality', Paper delivered at international conference 'New Directions in Islamic Thinking' held in Yogyakarta, 15–17 June 2004, p.1.

4. See for example the remarks made by Souad Saleh in her interview with *Al-Ahram Weekly*, 27 October – 2 November 2005, p. 27.

5. Other verses in the Qur'an that explicitly or implicitly mention the equality between men and women are: Q. 9.71,72, Q. 3.195, Q. 4.124, Q. 16.97, Q. 40.40 and Q. 48.5,6.

6. Brannon Wheeler, *Applying the Canon in Islam. The Authorization and Maintenance of Interpretive Reasoning in Hanafi Scholarship* New York, SUNY Press, 1996, p. 9.

7. Wheeler, *Applying*, p. 2,3.

8. Zainah Anwar, 'Gender Issues', p. 1 and 8.

9. For the type of hermeneutical work in Iran, see Ziba Mir-Hosseini, *Islam and*

Gender: The Religious Debate in Contemporary Iran, London and New York, 1999, for similar work in Indonesia, van Doorn-Harder, *Women Shaping Islam*. Highlighting the importance of re-interpreting the *fiqh* is among others Kecia Ali, 'Progressive Muslims and Islamic Jurisprudence: the Necessity for Critical Engagement with Marriage and Divorce Law', in ed. Omid Safi, *Progressive Muslims. On Justice, Gender, and Pluralism*, Oxford, Oneworld Publications, 2003, pp. 163–189 et al.

10. Mernissi's first book is still considered a classic: *Beyond the Veil: Male Female Dynamics in Modern Muslim Society*, Bloomington and Indianapolis, IN., 1975 and1987. Other famous books by Mernissi are *The Veil and the Male Elite: A Feminist Interpretation of Women's Rights in Islam*. (1987) Translated by Mary Jo Lakeland, Reading, Mass., 1991. *Women and Islam: An Historical and Theological Enquiry*, Oxford, 1991. Another seminal work by Mernissi is *Women's Rebellion and Islamic Memory*, London, Zed Books, 1996).

11. *Women and Islam*, p. 88, 89.

12. See for example her article 'The Muslim Concept of Active Female Sexuality' in Pinar Ilkkaracan, ed., *Women and Sexuality in Muslim Societies*, Istanbul, WWR, 2000.

13. Ibid., p. 34.

14. Riffat Hassan, 'An Islamic Perspective' in ed. Jeanne Becher, *Women, Religion and Sexuality*, Geneva, WCC Publications, 1991, p. 102.

15. Ibid., p. 104.

16. Riffat Hassan, 'Religious Human Rights in the Qur'an', in John Witte, Jr. and Johan D. van der Vijver, eds, The Hague, Martinus Nijhoff Publishers, 1996, p. 361. Also see her article in Gisela Webb, ed., *Windows of Faith. Muslim Women Scholar-Activists in North America*, Syracuse, NY, Syracuse University Press, 2000.

17. Ed. Forum Kajian Kitab Kuning (FK3), Wajah Baru Relasi Suami-Istri. Telaah Kitab `Uqud al-Lujjayn [The new face of the relation between man and wife. About the *Kitab Uqud*], Yogyakarta, LKiS, 2001,, p. X.

18. *Kitab 'Uqud al-Lujjain*, Surabaya, Bintang Terang, 1985, p. 24.

19. The entire exercise of the text's revision can be read in chapters 5 and 6 of my book *Women Shaping Islam*.

20. 'Gender Jihad' published at the Congress' website: http://www.feminismeislamic.org/eng/.

21. Among others, see: Abdennur Prado's article 'About the Friday Prayer led by Amina Wadud' http://www.studying-islam.org/articletext.aspx?id=955 & on www.webIslam.com.

22. *Al-Ahram Weekly* 27 October-2 November, 2005, p. 27.

Enlightened Interpretations of the
Hadith Literature

Hadith, which refers to the statements of the Prophet Muhammad, is the second source of law and theology in Islam after the Qur'an. Unlike the Qur'an, which is regarded by Muslims as containing verbatim the word of God as revealed to His prophet, the *hadith* literature for the most part does not convey the exact words of Muhammad but rather conveys their intended meaning. Most of the *hadith* which have come down to us were orally transmitted for a period of two to three centuries before they were committed to writing. The famous six books (Ar. *al-kutub al-sitta*) of *hadith* were compiled starting in the third/ninth century by al-Bukhari (870), Muslim b. al-Hajjaj (d. 875), Ibn Maja (d. 886), Abu Da'ud (d. 888), al-Tirmidhi (d. 892); and al-Nasa'i (d. 915). These are considered to be the most authoritative collections of *hadith* by the Sunnis. They have earned this status because the compilers, particularly al-Bukhari and Muslim, subjected the *hadiths* they had collected to stringent criteria in order to determine their reliability and sift fabricated reports away from the authentic ones. The criteria they invoked were mostly concerned with the moral probity and intellectual acumen of the *hadith* transmitters whose names occurred in the *isnads*. According to this science or discipline of *hadith* (Ar. *'ilm al-hadith*), three broad categories of *hadith* emerged: a. sound (Ar. *sahih*) – the best and most reliable *hadiths* whose *isnads* contained the names of reliable, pious transmitters; b. good (Ar. *hasan*) – almost equal in probative value to *sahih* reports except that one transmitter or more might have a slight character flaw; and c. weak (Ar. *da'if*) – when one or more transmitters are determined to be less than reliable in their narration on account of a character deficiency and/or faulty memory. There are further classifications of *hadith* based on the number of its transmitters and the extent of its dissemination, which need not concern us here. The Shi'a have their own compilations, which include not only prophetic statements but also the sayings of their Imams, their spiritual leaders after the death of the Prophet. This article will however focus only on Sunni interpretations of the *hadith* literature; Shi'i interpretations merit a special treatment which is beyond the purview of this article.[1]

In this article, I will briefly survey both pre-modern and modern interpretations of *hadith*, explore the connections between them, and describe some of the trends in the contemporary period which indicate a certain trajectory for future research and evolution.

Pre-Modern interpretations of *Hadith*

Within our length constraints, it would be impossible to do full justice to the range of perspectives that existed in the pre-modern period regarding *hadith* and its use as legal and theological proof-texts. At the risk of somewhat simplifying things, I will be discussing the following three broad periods in order: a. the earliest period of the Pious Forbears (Ar. *al-salaf al-salih*); b. the classical and medieval periods; and c. the late medieval period.

A. The period of the Pious Forbears

From most accounts it appears that *sunna* (referring to the 'custom' and 'practices' of the Prophet) was the more prevalent term in at least the first two centuries of Islam and used much more broadly than in the later period. In this early period *sunna*, besides meaning prophetic practice, referred additionally to the practices of the Companions (Ar. *al-Sahaba*). Thus, we have very early references to the *sunna* of the Prophet but also to the *sunnas* of the Rashidun caliphs Abu Bakr, 'Umar, and 'Uthman, as well as of others. In such usage, *sunna* meant more a moral exemplum rather than a specific practice or ruling of either the Prophet or his Companions.[2] In addition to or as a complement to *sunna*, we have in this early period the notion of *'amal* or 'living tradition', particularly of the Companions who lived in Medina and who were assumed to have authoritatively passed on details of the practices of the Prophet through their faithful emulation of his behavior.[3]

Over time however this broad meaning of *sunna* became progressively circumscribed so that it began to be restricted to that of *sunnat Muhammad* (practices of Muhammad) which eventually came to be codified in a text or statement (*hadith*) attributed to the Prophet. This development is already apparent in first/seventh century legal thought when the concepts of *hadith* and *isnad* in a religious-technical sense arose. The *isnad* refers to the chain of transmission of a *hadith* which records the names of its narrators while the actual text of the *hadith* is known as *matn*.

The need for articulating *sunna* in the form of a specific prophetic statement appears to have developed among the Successors, the second generation of Muslims. After the death of the Companions, knowledge and memory of the Prophet's statements were no longer as vivid and immediate for the next generation of his followers.[4] Thus one of the most famous Successors, the Umayyad caliph 'Umar b. 'Abd al-'Aziz (d. 101) commanded Abu Bakr al-Ansari and other scholars to 'look for what there is of the *hadith* of the Apostle and of his *sunna*'.[5] In this instance, *hadith* is already being used in the technical sense of a specific statement attributed to the Prophet and thus distinct from the broader term *sunna* referring to the collectivity of his actions.

B. The classical and medieval periods

From the third generation of Muslim scholars, the early jurists Malik b. Anas (d. 796) and al-Shafi'i (d. 802) contributed the most to streamlining these critical concepts and detailing the use of *hadith* and *sunna* as legal proof-texts. Malik, the eponymous founder of the Maliki school of law, is the author of *al-Muwatta* ('The Well-Trodden Path'), a collection of primarily legal *hadiths*, whose excellence has been widely recognized. Some scholars have even been inclined to count the *Muwatta* as part of the six authoritative *hadith* collections instead of the *Sunan* of Ibn Maja. For Malik, the value of *hadith* lay not in providing a specific legal ruling but in indicating how specific rules should be applied. He also made considerable use of the living tradition or practices of the people of Medina (Ar. *'amal*), understood to be based on the Prophet's *sunna*, as the basis for legal rulings.[6]

Malik's student, al-Shafi'i insisted, however, that *sunna* could serve as a source of law only if it was codified in a *hadith*. *Hadith* texts provided the basis for legal decisions. Al-Shafi'i further maintained that the consensus of Muslim scholars, regardless of how universal it was, could not create a legal ruling in the absence of a specific *hadith* to support it. This legal methodology developed by al-Shafi'i proved to be very influential through time and remains so till today, despite the fact that the Shafi'i legal school today is far less prevalent than it used to be, having lost ground to the Hanafi school under the Ottomans.[7]

While the status of *hadith* as legal proof-texts rose among jurists and scholars in general starting in the second/eighth century, one early group of scholars resisted this trend. The Mu'tazila, who are usually described as scholastic or rationalist theologians, retained a highly skeptical attitude toward the authenticity and, therefore, the reliability of *hadith* as proof-texts in legal or theological dialectics.[8] Some of the criticism they leveled at the *hadith* scholars (Ar. *muhaddithun*) may sound remarkably modern to us. An example of such a critical Mu'tazili scholar is Amr b. Bahr al-Jahiz (d. 869), the famous polymath of the third/ninth century who criticized the use of certain 'praise' reports (*fada'il or manaqib*) whose texts were clearly tendentious and contradictory, as proof-texts in Sunni-Shi'i dialectics. These dialectics had centered on determining whether Abu Bakr (the first caliph) or 'Ali (the fourth caliph) was the most qualified to become the leader of the community. In the following remarks addressed to his Shi'i interlocutors, he expresses his exasperation over the fact that both sides are equally able to produce reports which confirm the right of one over the other to rule:

> If what you related regarding the excellence of Ali is true, and what they have related regarding the excellence of Abu Bakr is true, then Abu Bakr is more excellent than 'Ali and 'Ali is more excellent than Abu Bakr. This, then, is the contradiction but the truth is never contradictory. In this is proof that the Prophet, God's blessings and peace be upon him, did not speak of this or mention that, for if a report emanates in a general way with regard to the superiority of Abu Bakr, and likewise with regard to the superiority of 'Ali, then it is of no value except for what we said to the effect that the Prophet, peace and blessings be upon him, said one of the two statements for which attestation may be found, and did not utter the other [statement]; that rather it [sc. the other] was invented by men, and fabricated by the transmitters of biographical material[9]

Al-Jahiz then states that independent attestation for the reliability of such praise reports should be sought in alternate evidentiary texts such as historical reports, biographical narratives, and even early poetry. His views on seeking confirmation (*tathabbut*) of the truth are based on 'man's need to investigate this world of reason and harmony which God has placed at his disposal and for his instruction . . . .'[10] Rational inquiry of this sort makes it possible to dispense with the elaborate criteria devised by the *hadith* scholars to ascertain the reliability of reports. Al-Jahiz, like other Mu 'tazili scholars, was thus not overly reliant on the categories developed by *hadith* scholars to organize knowledge. He was rather more concerned with the concepts of the possible (*al-ja'iz*) and impossible (*al-mumtani*), and to reject reports based on their inner contradictions and implausibility.[11] In determining the reliability of traditions, conformity to historical facts was a far more important criterion for al-Jahiz than traditional *isnad* criticism.

Al-Jahiz was moreover of the opinion that partisan quibbling over the meaning of the words of specific reports has resulted from the ignorance of later generations of the actual circumstances of the uttering of prophetic statements (Ar. *asbab wurud al-hadith*), leading them to derive a general meaning from a more specific one. This is easily conducive to faulty application of legal rulings.[12] The general Mu'tazili skepticism towards *hadith* has enjoyed a resurgence among some modernist Muslims, as will be discussed below.

C. The Late Medieval Period

From after the twelfth century as the Mu'tazila faded away, a fairly conservative attitude towards *hadith* took hold among scholars which continues until today. In general, the tendency has been to accept all *hadith* contained in the two *sahih* collections of al-Bukhari and Muslim in particular as sound, whose contents are normative for Muslims. The prevailing belief is that the necessary work of sifting and evaluation of *hadiths* has already been painstakingly completed by irreproachable scholars. There is no need, therefore, to subject them to critical scrutiny again and thereby cast doubt on the integrity of scholars such as al-Bukhari and Muslim. In the view of most traditionalist *'ulama'*, once a *hadith* has been labeled and acknowledged as 'sound' by the consensus of prominent scholars, then it should be accepted as such by believing Muslims. Verified, sound *hadiths* in fact came to be regarded as a revealed source second only to the Qur'an in importance.

An important dissenting voice in the fourteenth century was that of Ibn Khaldun (d. 1382), the famous historian who remarked:

Historians, [Qur'anic] interpreters, and leading transmitters have often fallen into error by accepting [the authenticity of certain] reports and incidents. This is because they relied only on the transmission, whether of value or worthless. They did not [carefully] inspect [these reports] in light of [fundamental] principles [of historical analysis] or compare the reports to each other or examine them according to the standards of wisdom or investigate the nature of beings.[13]

There was however to a lesser extent critical scrutiny of the contents of *hadith*. Textual analysis was resorted to particularly in the case of spurious reports or reports likely to be spurious, such as the *fada'il* ('praise') ones. The imperative for engaging in textual criticism in such cases may be seen to be established in the following statement by the scholar al-Suyuti (d. 911/1505): 'If you encounter a *adith* contrary to reason, or to what has been established as correctly reported, or against the accepted principles, then you should know that it is forged.'[14] In response to the question whether a *hadith*'s spuriousness may be detected without resorting to *isnad* criticism, the famous Hanbali scholar Ibn Qayyim al-Jawziyya (d. 751/1350) lauds the question as one of momentous significance (*'azim al-qadr*) and then proceeds to state that it is so possible for the scholar, who besides a thorough acquaintance and long familiarity with *hadith* (which creates in him a 'sixth sense' [*dhawq*], so to speak, for gauging reliability), also possesses knowledge about the biographical details of the Prophet's life, his conduct, his speech, and what may credibly be ascribed to him or not.[15] Veridicality was, therefore, a fairly important, although not consistent, consideration in the assessment of the overall reliability of the texts of various kinds of reports in the pre-modern period.

Modernist and Reformist Attitudes toward *Hadith*

A highly critical and even skeptical attitude toward *hadith* developed in the nineteenth century among a number of reformist and modernist Muslim scholars, in some measure due to the debilitating consequences of European colonization of large portions of the Islamic world. The colonial and post-colonial conditions have induced much soul-searching among learned Muslims and a critical reevaluation of their intellectual heritage. The giant among such scholars in the nineteenth century was the Egyptian theologian Muhammad 'Abduh (d. 1905). He was a brilliant, erudite man who was a student of another pioneering reformist Jamal al-Din al-Afghani (d. 1897) and served as the rector of famed al-Azhar University in Cairo, Egypt. 'Abduh encouraged Muslims to revive their earlier tradition of critical inquiry and focus it, *inter alia*, on the *hadith* literature. Influenced to a certain extent by earlier Mu'tazili skepticism towards *hadith*, he even encouraged interrogating the reliability of sound reports when necessary, stressing that these were categories created by fallible human beings and, therefore, subject to reevaluation on the basis of rational criteria. He regarded the widespread acceptance of spurious *hadiths* as having contributed to the adoption of non-Islamic practices by Muslims and having led to the corruption of their beliefs and their internal disunity.[16] As might be expected, such positions were considered quite controversial in his time and his project never got fully underway. But 'Abduh at least planted the seeds of a reformist enterprise which continued to be taken up sporadically by modernists in the following century.

Arguably the most important of twentieth century modernists is Fazlur Rahman (d. 1988), who was a professor of Islamic Studies and then the Harold H. Swift Distinguished Service Professor at the University of Chicago until his death. Rahman's views on the *hadith* literature were in many ways an extension of 'Abduh's. He similarly urged Muslims to use *hadiths* more critically after having duly learned about their provenance and their reliability and not simply abide by the traditional system of classification. He also stressed that *hadith* criticism should not remain as focused on *isnad* criticism as in the medieval period and that the texts (*mutun*) of *hadiths* should be inspected for veridicality. Even if the *isnads* of certain *hadiths* were spurious, he argued, their content may have a bearing on certain matters in the contemporary period, and thus still prove useful.[17] Rahman firmly believed that a properly conceived critique of *hadith* would lead to 'fresh thinking about Islam'.[18]

Future Trajectory

Modernist and reformist scholars of different stripes today continue the methodological and textual critiques initiated by their predecessors. In addition to *isnad* criticism, critical scrutiny of texts to determine their veridicality and historicity undergirds much of their methodology. If the texts of *hadiths* are at variance with Qur'anic prescriptions, the modernists tend to discount the *hadiths* in favor of the relevant Qur'anic verses. This is particularly evident in discussions of the *hudud* penalties, which are mostly derived from the *hadith* and in some cases are contrary to Qur'anic rulings. Thus, modernists point out that stoning or any form of capital punishment is not mentioned in the Qur'an at all but is derived only from the *hadith* literature, a fact which invites revisitation of the *hudud* laws.[19] Discriminatory attitudes towards women partly arose on account of some *hadiths* which describe Eve (Ar. *Hawwa'*) as having been fashioned out of Adam's rib and, therefore, endowed with an essentially 'crooked' nature. Furthermore some reports occurring particularly in exegetical literature blame Eve for having caused the banishment of humans from Paradise. In both cases these reports depart completely from the text of the Qur'an since the latter has no mention of Adam's rib or of its function in fundamentally shaping woman's nature. Furthermore, the Qur'an either equally blames Adam and his wife (2.30–39; 7.11–27) or Adam alone for the Fall (20.115–124) and does not single out Eve as the culprit in this incident. However, most late medieval male exegetes came to prefer reports that blame Eve, even though they were of dubious reliability and clearly show biblical influence, over the Qur'anic creation accounts, since the former suited their sensibilities much better in the patriarchal societies they now inhabited.[20]

Modernists and reformists in general are calling for a reevaluation of much of the *hadith* literature and an increased emphasis on the Qur'an to counteract the misogyny and violation of human rights that have frequently resulted from a non-critical acceptance of selected *hadiths*.[21] There is also a concerted effort to revive the pre-Shafi'i wholistic concept of *sunna* which included both prophetic praxis and speech. The Prophet Muhammad's performance of domestic chores and marriage to divorced or widowed middle-aged women, as widely reported in biographical sources, for example, can then be upheld as normative examples for Muslim men, even though these actions may not have received validation through impeccably documented *hadiths* counseling the adoption of such practices. There is also renewed interest in focusing on the 'causes for the appearance of *hadiths*', as recommended by al-Jahiz in the third/ninth century, since probing into the historical provenance of a *hadith* has much to tell us about the normative applicability of its text.[22] The brilliant fourteenth century jurist, Abu Ishaq al-Shatibi (d. 790/1388), who finds much favor with modernists, empha-sized that 'no individual text by itself can have absolute probative force unless it is understood in the light of its historical background and the total relevant teaching of the Qur'an and the Sunna'.[23]

These trajectories of scholarly inquiry and critique currently underway allow one to be cautiously optimistic for the future of *hadith* studies. With a critical mass of Muslim scholars now engaged in such an enterprise, they promise to yield highly beneficial results with possibly startling conse-quences for the reshaping of Islamic thought and the remaking of Islamic societies.

Notes

1. For a comparison of Sunni and Shi'i use of a select group of *hadith* as proof-texts particularly in debates regarding legitimate leadership of the Muslim community, see my book *Excellence and Precedence*, Leiden, E.J. Brill, 2002, pp. 197–228.

2. See Wael Hallaq, *A History of Islamic Legal Theories: An Introduction to Sunni Usul al-Fiqh*, Cambridge, Cambridge University Press, 1997, p. 12.

3. See Yasin Dutton, *The Origins of Islamic Law: the Qur'an, the Muwatta and Madinan 'Amal*, Surrey, Curzon, 1999.

4. Hallaq, *History*, p. 14.

5. Nabia Abbott, *Studies in Arabic Literary Papyri*, Chicago, University of Chicago Press, 1972, p. 2:26.

6. See further, Dutton, *Origins, passim*; Muhammad Hashim Kamali, *Principles of Islamic Jurisprudence*, Cambridge, Islamic Texts Society, 1991, pp. 283–96.

7. For a general introduction to this jurist's life and thought, see al-Shafi'i, *Islamic Jurisprudence: Shafi'i's Risala*, tr. Majid Khadduri, Baltimore, Johns Hopkins University Press, 1961, Introduction.

8. On this tendency of the Muctazila, see Schacht, *Origins of Muhammadan Jurisprudence*, Oxford, Clarendon Press, 1953, pp. 258–59; 'Abd al-Majid, *al-Ittijahat al-fiqhiyya 'inda ashab al-hadith*, Cairo, Maktabat al-Khanji, 1979, p. 94.

9. Al-Jahiz, *Kitab al-'Uthmaniyya*, ed. 'Abd al-Salam Muhammad Harun, Cairo, Dar al-Kitab al-'Arabi, 1955, p. 37–38.

10. Tarif Khalidi, *Arabic Historical Thought in the Classical Period*, Cambridge, Cambridge University Press, pp. 104–5.

11. See his *Kitab al-Hayawan*, ed. 'Abd al-Salam Muhammad Harun, Cairo, al-Maktaba al-Hamidiyya al-Misriyya, 1965–9, pp. 238–39; Khalidi, *Arabic Historical Thought*, pp. 106–7.

12. *'Uthmaniyya*, pp. 158–59.

13. Ibn Khaldun, *al-Muqaddima*, Beirut, Dar Ihya al-Turath, n.d., pp. 9–10; quoted by Khaled Abou el Fadl, *Speaking in God's Name: Islamic Law, Authority and Women*, Oxford, OneWorld, 2001, p. 110

14. Al-Suyuti, *Tadrib al-rawi*, Cairo, 1307/1889, p. 100; Muhammad Zubayr Siddiqi, *Hadith Literature: Its Origin, Development & Special Features*, ed. Abdal Hakim Murad, Cambridge, Islamic Texts Society, 1993, p. 113.

15. Ibn Qayyim al-Jawziyya, *al-Manar al-munif al-sahih wa-'l-da'if*, ed. Abd al-Fattah Abu Ghudda, Aleppo, 1390/1970.

16. See Mazheruddin Siddiqi, *Modern Reformist Thought in the Muslim World*, Islamabad, Islamic Research Institute, 1982, pp. 67, 102–3; David Commins, *Islamic Reform: Politics and Social Change in Late Ottoman Syria*, New York, Oxford University Press, 1990, p. 31. For a broader introduction to 'Abduh's thought and activism and of his mentor, al-Afghani, see Albert Hourani, *Arabic Thought in the*

Liberal Age: 1798–1939, Cambridge, Cambridge University Press, 1983, pp. 103–244.

17. Fazlur Rahman, *Islamic Methodology in History*, Karachi, 1965, Chapter 2.

18. Fazlur Rahman, *Islam and Modernity*, Chicago, University of Chicago Press, 1982, p. 147.

19. See, for example, Mohamed Talbi, "Religious Liberty," in *Liberal Islam: A Sourcebook*, ed. Charles Kurzman, Oxford, Oxford University Press,1998, 161–68.

20. For this fascinating discussion, see Barbara Freyer Stowasser, *Women in the Qur'an, Traditions, and Interpretation*, Oxford, 1994, 'The Chapter of Eve', pp. 25–38.

21. See, for example, Abou el Fadl, *Speaking*, passim; Fatima Mernissi, *The Veil and the Male Elite: A Feminist Interpretation of Women's Rights in Islam*, tr. Mary Jo Lakeland, Reading, Addison-Wesley Publishing Company, 1991.

22. See my '*Asbab Wurud al-Hadith*: Historicizing the Speech of the Prophet Muhammad', article in progress, for an abbreviated draft version of it, see www.yale.edu/cir/2003/afsaruddinpaper.doc.

23. Rahman, *Islam and Modernity*, p. 25.

Turkish Islam in Dialogue with Modern Society
The Neo-Sufi Spirituality of the
Gülen Movement

THOMAS MICHEL

I. The need for a modern spirituality

The emergence in recent years in Europe and North America of interest in the thought of Turkish scholar Fethullah Gülen is a phenomenon that demands explanation. Several American universities, such as Georgetown and Rice, have held academic seminars to study the various aspects of his thought. In the Netherlands alone, at least four universities (Nijmegen, Tilburg, Erasmus in Rotterdam, and Amsterdam) have hosted seminars on 'Forerunners for Peace', which prominently featured the views of Gülen and his movement.

Several factors have contributed to this interest. Firstly, people who feel oppressed by the materialist and consumerist character of modern life are looking for a spirituality that can point a way to live authentically and usefully, and many find such spirituality in the writings and movement of Fethullah Gülen. Secondly, Muslims seeking a way to live their Islamic faith in modern situations and make a positive contribution to the transformation of society find in the movement a constructive interpretation of Qur'anic teaching that stresses good deeds and service to humanity. Thirdly, non-Muslims who are looking for Muslim partners with whom they can live and work together, share ideas, and form friendships find in the Gülen movement ethically concerned individuals who are open to cooperate in building pluralist societies and working for peace, justice, and human development. In this article, I will focus on the Sufi-oriented spirituality that Mr Gülen proposes for his followers.

A recent survey of Europeans reports a decreasing interest in 'religion' among respondents, but a corresponding increase of interest in 'spirituality'.

At first glance, this seems inconsistent, but it reflects a widespread and typical modern attitude. When people express disinterest in 'religion', I believe that they are referring to traditional ritual, which they consider, perhaps based on unhappy childhood memories, to be dry, formalistic, preachy, but empty of deeper meaning. Conversely, their interest in 'spirituality' reflects the need they feel for some form of contact with the Divine in their lives. They are dissatisfied with a purely positivist approach to life and are seeking transcendent input, insights originating from outside the closed circle of modern society and culture, a spiritual discipline which can help one progress on the path of personal interior growth and transformation.

Sufism, the generally accepted term for the Islamic mystical tradition, is seen by some as providing such food for the spirit. Sufism is not a single clearly defined movement, but an interrelated network of ideas and practices aimed at a deeper understanding and faithful pursuit of the Qur'anic message. Scholars, as well as Sufis themselves, who attempt to give a succinct definition of Sufism inevitably pull out certain elements that have been emphasized by some Sufis at certain periods of history, while disregarding or glossing over other characteristics that do not fit in and perhaps even contradict their definition.[1]

For some, it is *asceticism* and simplicity of life that is the key to a true following of Islam. Others emphasize *love* as the central idea and understand the Sufi path as one leading to a union of love with God, the Beloved. For others, Sufism is a voluntarist path by which the believer, by concentrating on virtue and moral behavior, comes into a union of *will* with God, a state in which the mystic seeks only to do the will of God. Many mystics see the Path as primarily one of intuitive *knowledge*, of becoming aware of the eternal Truth, the perennial wisdom of the heart that is the only sure font of true insight. Still others affirm the *oneness of all existence*, so that the mystical path is essentially a psychological growth in awareness that the believer, as well as all that goes to make up the cosmos, is simply a transient manifestation of the One, the unique existing being. Some Sufis emphasize extraordinary mystical *experience*, expressed in states of ecstasy, inspired utterances, visions, and dreams; for others the path is a contemplative *pilgrimage* to God residing in the silent cave of the heart, and for still others, it is a path of *service* and concern for humankind.

II. Fethullah Gülen and Sufism

Those unacquainted with the background of Fethullah Gülen can find much information about him, his writings, and his movement on several well-maintained internet websites.[2] In my article on Gülen as educator[3], I briefly trace the origins of the movement associated with his name. Born in eastern Turkey in 1941, he completed religious studies in a *madrasa* in Erzurum and began teaching in 1958. The movement arose some years later in Izmir, in the 1960s, among a small group of like-minded educators and students, and it is from this nucleus of educators that the movement has grown. It is estimated that the movement embraces, with varying degrees of involvement, between two and four million Muslims and runs over 300 schools in more than 30 countries. In Turkey, the movement owns publishing houses, a daily newspaper and television channel. Operating independently, but maintaining links of coordination and training, the schools and *dershanes* are a loose federation of educational institutions that share a common pedagogic vision, similar curriculum, and human and material resources.

In a study of 'the neo-Sufi spirituality of the Gülen movement', the obvious place to begin is whether 'Khoja effendi', as he is affectionately called by his followers and associates, is a Sufi. Gülen has had to defend his movement several times from the accusation that he has founded a new Sufi order, of which he is the *shaykh*.[4] In Turkey today, the charge of founding a secret *tarekat* (*tariqa*) carries ideological weight as well as legal and political implications. Secular modernists view Sufism as part of the pre-modern past, a relic from Ottoman times, an obstacle to progress, development and prosperity. Conversely, Muslim activists of *salafi* tendency accuse Sufism of being responsible for introducing unwarranted and unorthodox innovations into Islam and for promulgating a passive, pietistic religiosity.

Gülen denies that he has founded a *tarekat* and underscores that he has never belonged to any Sufi order. He states: 'The religious orders are institutions that appeared six centuries after our Prophet in the name of representing Sufism. They have their own rules and structures. Just as I never joined a Sufi order, I have never had any relationship with one.'[5] To the question of why he is called *Khoja*, (literally: 'Teacher') a form of address traditionally used by Sufis for their master, he answers that the title carries no hierarchical, organizational, or Ottoman revivalist connotation, but is simply 'a respectful way of addressing someone whose knowledge on religious matters is recognized and acknowledged by the general public.'[6]

Given that Gülen has never belonged to a *tarekat*, is it still accurate to regard him as a Sufi? In a seminal work on Sufi elements in Gülen's thought, Zeki Saritoprak[7] calls Gülen 'a Sufi in his own way.' Saritoprak affirms that many Sufis belonged to no Sufi Order. For the first six centuries of Islam, there were no Sufi Orders, yet there were many important Sufis. Even after the appearance of Sufi orders in the thirteenth and fourteenth centuries, there are instances of well-known Sufis who did not belong to any *tarekat*.

Yet the appearance of the 'independent Sufi' has usually been considered anomalous by traditional Sufi adepts. On the one hand, by belonging to no Order, the independent Sufi forgoes the established guidance and discipline set down by one of the great *shaykhs* of the past and thereby runs the risk of wandering aimlessly on the spiritual path; on the other hand, by not placing trust in a *pir*, a spiritual director, the Sufi is liable to be deceived by Satan or by his own whims. Saritoprak notes that although Islamic history gives many examples of great Sufis who have 'followed their own paths', the situation of the modern Sufi who follows no *tarekat* and has no spiritual guide is considered problematic.

Early Sufis had neither orders nor even Sufi organizations. Rabia, Junayd, Muhasibi, Bishr, Ghazzali, Feriduddin Attar, and even Rumi did not belong to a *tariqah*. However, they were Sufis. From the vantage point of institutionalized Sufism, their Sufism would be problematic, because these early Sufis did not have a spiritual master. In the Sufi tradition, he who has no a *shaykh*, finds Satan as his *shaykh*.[8]

It is true that the vast majority of Sufis have discouraged or even forbidden one from following the Sufi path without a *shaykh/pir*. However, a minority view holds that the spiritual guide need not be a living person. Kharaqani, for example, was initiated into the Sufi path by the spirit of Abu Yazid al-Bistami, while 'Attar was inspired by the spirit of Al-Hallaj. Other Sufis have claimed as their guide Khidr, the mysterious companion of Moses whose story is recounted in the Qur'an in Surat al-Kahf.

Gülen's position is that he is guided in his spiritual development by the Qur'an and the *sunna*. He holds that the Qur'an is not only the best guide, but is the source and font of all Sufi thought and practice. Rooted in the Qur'an and *sunna*, and supplemented by the views and experiences of later Sufis down through the centuries who applied the Qur'anic teachings through their own personal efforts (*ijtihad*), Sufism must not be considered an 'alternative' path followed by some Muslims in contradiction to the *shari'a*, but should be regarded as one of the basic sciences of Islam. It 'is not contradictory with any of the Islamic ways found in the Book and the *Sunna*; far from being contradictory, it has its source, like the other religious sciences, in the Book and the *Sunna* and the conclusions drawn from the Qur'an and *Sunna* by conscientious scholars of the early period of Islam.[9]

For Gülen, *tasawwuf* and *shari'a* are two ways of expressing the same truth. The two forms of expression arise from differences in personality rather than from any contradictory messages. Both lead the Muslim to believe and practice the one Islamic truth, but each Muslim must find the path most suited to his disposition. Sufism has known antinomian Sufis who claimed that following the exoteric (*zahir*) regulations of the *shari'a* were unnecessary for those on the esoteric (*batin*) path, but Gülen is clearly among those who stress the importance for the Sufi to not abandon the *shari'a*. In this, he exemplifies the long line of *shari'a*-oriented Sufis, represented most strongly by the Qadiri and Naqshbandi *tarekat*, and in modern times by Said Nursi, who regard *tasawwuf* as the interiorized facet of the life of the sincere Muslim who seeks to live fully the message contained in the Qur'an and sunna.[10]

III. The influence of Said Nursi

Ozdalga sees three 'positive reference points' which have shaped Gülen's thinking: 1) orthodox Sunni Islam, 2) the Naqshbandi Sufi tradition, 3) the Nurculuk movement, that is, those Muslims influenced by the writings of Said Nursi.[11] The Naqshbandis have always insisted on the careful performance of the prescriptions of the *shari'a*, so there is no contradiction between the first two points. Gülen differs from the Naqshbandi Order however in that the Naqshbandi disciple is presented with an explicit program of spiritual development, which is closely monitored by the *shaykh*, whereas Gülen's approach is more open-ended and stresses good deeds and service to humanity (*hizmet*) more than spiritual exercises and devotions.

Probably the most important formative influence on the development of Gülen's thought, including his approach to Sufism, was Said Nursi.[12] Like Nursi, whose training was also within the Naqshbandi tradition but who chose to work and teach outside the confines of an established *tarekat*[13], so also Gülen sees the Sufi tradition more as the accumulated wisdom of the saints of Islam, rather than an institutional necessity for internalizing Islamic values.

Moreover, like Said Nursi, Gülen is aware that not everything that historically has passed in the name of Sufism is of positive value. A critical approach to the Sufi tradition however must recognize the intrinsic strength of the movement as an instrument for fostering and building a sense of community and brotherhood. Nursi states: 'The Sufi path may not be condemned because of the evils of certain ways which have adopted practices outside the bounds of *taqwa*, and even of Islam, and have wrongfully given themselves the name of Sufi paths. Quite apart from the important and elevated religious and spiritual results of the Sufi path . . . it is the Sufi paths which are the first and most effective and fervent means of expanding and developing brotherhood, a sacred bond within the World of Islam.'[14]

IV. The inner dimension of religion

Gülen understands Sufism as the inner dimension of the *shari'a*, and the two dimensions must never be separated. Performance of the externals without attention to their interior transformative power results in dry ritualism. Conversely, a concentration on interior discipline while rejecting prescribed ritual can reduce the spiritual path to that of following one's own preferences and proclivities. Only by activating both dimensions of Islam will the seeker be able to humbly submit one's life fully to God.[15]

Just as Sufism 'brings to life the religious sciences', in Al-Ghazali's phrase, so the *shari'a* keeps the believer rooted in the Islamic tradition. 'If the traveler has not been able to prepare his heart according to both the requirements of his spiritual journeying and the commandments of the Shari'a, that is, if he does not think and reason in the light of Prophethood while his feelings fly in the boundless realm of his spiritual state, he will inevitably fall. He will be confused and bewildered, speaking and acting contrary to the spirit of the Shari'a.'[16]

Gülen defines Sufism as 'the path followed by an individual who, having been able to free himself or herself from human vices and weaknesses in order to acquire angelic qualities and whose conduct is pleasing to God, lives in accordance with the requirements of God's knowledge and love and in the resulting spiritual delight that ensues.'[17] It is evident that Gülen falls within the voluntarist approach to Sufi spirituality, giving priority to the will, emphasizing the overcoming of human obstacles to God's power and grace, and acquiring the virtues and behavior that God desires in His servants.[18]

The *murid* who draws near to a union of will with God is inevitably growing as well in *ma'rifa* or spiritual wisdom, in love (*mahabba*, *'ishq*) for God and for others, and is confirmed in his or her path by the gift of spiritual joy. Gülen's understanding is consistent with the mainstream of Sufi teaching, according to which the Sufi exerts his or her own efforts to attain the spiritual stations (*maqamat*), thereby removing one by one the obstacles to divine grace, and then waits trustfully for God to grant as gifts the spiritual states (*ahwal*) of knowledge, love, and delight.

Gülen observes that the Muslims who, down through the centuries, have most reflected upon and sought to practice the interior values taught by Islam and who developed the spiritual disciplines for controlling selfish impulses, were in fact Sufis.

> As a religion, Islam naturally emphasizes the spiritual realm. It takes the training of the ego as a basic principle. Asceticism, piety, kindness and sincerity are essential. In the history of Islam, the discipline that dwelt most on these matters was Sufism.[19]

V. The basis for a modern spirituality

Gülen sees the importance of Sufism for a modern Islamic spirituality in providing a program of discipline by which the believer can come to renounce both consumerist tendencies and secular heedlessness. This renunciation is not empty asceticism for its own sake, but is oriented toward the greater reward of becoming aware of spiritual realities. For Gülen, as al-Ghazali had previously discovered, Sufism brings the blessing of an experiential confirmation of faith assertions that had previously been only intellectually apprehended. Gülen explains:

> Sufism enables individuals to deepen their awareness of themselves as devotees of God. Through the renunciation of this transient, material world and the desires and emotions it engenders, they awaken to the reality of the other world, which is turned toward God's Beautiful Names. Sufism allows individuals to develop the moral dimension of one's existence, and enables the acquisition of a strong, heartfelt, and personally experienced conviction of the articles of faith that before had only been accepted superficially.[20]

In short, the genius of Sufism, according to Gülen, is its ability to *interiorize* the message of the Qur'an so that it influences and shapes the behavior

of the Muslim. Through Sufism, the Muslim learns to move beyond obey-
ing commands and regulations that he or she does not understand to an
appreciation of Islamic teaching which becomes part and parcel of the
believer's way of life. Sufism shows how a Muslim can overcome selfish
tendencies, respond to frustration and opposition, and with patience and
perseverance move beyond discouragement and routine. Sufism leads the
way to *shawq*, delight, so that religious commitment is not some onerous and
unpleasant burden that a person is forced to carry, but can be conducive to a
joyful, loving acceptance of life before God.

For Gülen, Sufism is its ability to offer a practical program by which the
Muslim can internalize Islamic faith so that it motivates a life of service to
humankind. He shows little interest in the ecstatic or para-normal mystical
experiences sometimes claimed by or for Sufi saints, and he criticizes the
way Sufi teaching and practice has been handed down in the past century.
Despite the decadent state in which Sufi thought and practice is often being
handed down, he affirms that a renewed approach to the Sufi tradition can
enrich still Muslim spirituality and offer direction for the future. If a pre-
condition for the progress of civilization is the changing of outdated and
ineffective mentalities[21], this is only achieved when one acknowledges his
own limitations, recognizes the need for controlling his impulses, and finds
motivation to strive for virtue and knowledge. This is what Sufism is all
about: 'The Islamic spiritual life based on asceticism, regular worship,
abstention from all major and minor sins, sincerity and purity of intention,
love and yearning, and the individual's admission of his essential impotence
and destitution became the subject-matter of Sufism.'[22]

The Sufi training, as a discipline which highlights the inner dimension
of Islamic teaching, enables the Muslim to confront critically but with
moderation the challenges of modernity without falling into the snares
either of unreflective acceptance or angry refusal. Gülen's Sufi-oriented
spirituality is an attempt to respond to the fundamental questions faced by
all conscientious modern believers: how to develop humane qualities, good
behavior, love for others, enthusiasm for self-improvement, and an active
desire to serve others, to make a difference in the world, and to persevere in
this desire in the face of setbacks and failures. According to Gülen, in the
Islamic tradition it is the Sufi thinkers who have thought through these
questions and have developed experimental methods for dealing with them,
and he consequently continues to propose this spiritual research as useful for
his followers.

Notes

1. Anne-Marie Schimmel, in her treatment *What is Sufism?* never attempts a comprehensive definition, but rather cites the various descriptions of Sufism given by Sufis and scholars. For example, Ruwaym's description: 'The Sufis are people who prefer God to everything and God prefers them to everything else.' *Mystical Dimensions of Islam*, Chapel Hill, University of North Carolina Press, 1975, p. 15.

2. www.fethullahgulen.org/, www.fgulen.com/, www.thelightpublishing.com/ writer.php?id=1, http://www.fountainmagazine.com/index.php are few of the main sites in English.

3. Thomas Michel, 'Fethullah Gülen as Educator', *Turkish Islam and the Secular State*, Syracuse:, Syracuse U.P., 2003, pp. 69–70.

4. Ibid., p. 83.

5. Fethullah Gülen, cited in L.E. Webb, *Fethullah Gülen: Is There More to Him than Meets the Eye?*, Patterson, N.J., Zinnur Books, 1983, p. 103.

6. Ibid., p. 80.

7. Zeki Saritoprak, 'Fethullah Gülen: A Sufi in His Own Way', *Turkish Islam*, pp.156–169. Saritoprak's paper is the first to study the Sufi elements in Gülen's thought; I will try not to repeat what he has stated.

8. Saritoprak, p. 160.

9. F. Gülen, *Key Concepts in the Practice of Islam*, Izmir, Kaynak, 1997, p. 9.

10. Ihsan Yülmaz notes: 'Most scholars agree that 'Gülen continues a long Sufi tradition of seeking to address the spiritual needs of people, to educate the masses, and to provide some stability in times of turmoil'. 'Ihsan Yülmaz, citing Ebru Altünolu, *Fethullah Gülen's Perception of State and Society*, Istanbul, Milliyet Yayünlar, 1999, p. 102, in '*Ijtihad* and *Tajdid* by Conduct: The Gülen Movement', *Turkish Islam*, p. 228.

11. Elisabeth Özdalga, 'Worldly Asceticism in Islamic Casting: Fethullah Gülen's Inspired Piety and Activism', *Critique* 17 (2000), p. 91.

12. In his commentary on Nursi's treatise, *The Epitomes of Light*, Gülen refers to Said Nursi as 'the Master' and urges that his works be studied in depth.

13. Said Nursi, *Letters*, Twenty-ninth Letter, Ninth Section, First Allusion, Istanbul, Sozler, 1997, p. 518.

14. Said Nursi, *Letters*, Twenty-ninth Letter, Ninth Section, Third Allusion, p. 521.

15. Fethullah Gülen, 'Sufism and Its Origins', *The Fountain*, July-September, 1999.

16. Fethullah Gülen, 'Key Concepts in the Practice of Sufism', p. 190.

17. Fethullah Gülen, *Sufism*, trans. Ali Unal, Istanbul, Fountain, 1999, p. xiv.

18. 'Such a transformation results in God's directing the individual's will in accordance with His will.' F. Gülen, *Toward a Global Civilization of Love and Tolerance*, Somerset, NJ, The Light, 2004, p. 164.

19. Gülen, cited in Webb, p. 103.
20. Fethullah Gülen, *Advocate of Dialogue*, Fairfax, VA, Fountain, 2000, p. 352.
21. Fethullah Gülen, *Towards the Lost Paradise*, p. 71.
22. Fethullah Gülen, *Criteria or Lights of the Way I*, Izmir, Kaynak, 1998, p. 50.

Humanism and Islam
The Contribution of three
Erasmus Prize Laureates 2004

ERIK BORGMAN

In 2004 the Praemium Erasmianum Foundation for the first time since its founding in 1958 awarded the Erasmus Prize to 'three vehicles of culture from the Islamic culture area'. Through 'their open and critical attitude and their enlightened patterns of thought with regard to religion and society' they represented a good connection with 'the ideas of Erasmus whose name the award bears'.[1] The Foundation awards the prize in the context of the 'intellectual debate between religion and modernity'. Here the question is asked 'what is the position of religion with regard to processes of modernization in society such as the development of increased knowledge, secularization, individualization and democratization'. The answer to the question as to 'whether religion is an obstacle to modernization' as is hinted at here is not just 'yes', as it seems to have become more and more common since the 11 September 2001. The Foundation asks to engage with the idea 'that processes of modernization may not always develop according to models developed in the west.'[2] The three Muslim intellectuals whom the Praemium Erasmianum Foundation has moved into the lime light will enable us in this article to access the debate within Islam with regard to the relationship between religion and modernity and about the special contribution which religion makes to modernity. The particular kind of humanism which they represent deserves to be listened in the debates on this subject.

The Erasmus laureate of 2004 best known in the West is without a doubt Fatema Mernissi (born in 1940 in Fez). A scholar of political science and sociology, she studied *inter alia* in Rabat and Paris and now teaches at the Muhammed V. University of Arbat. She became famous through her writings about life in a harem, a disappearing world in which she had still grown up, through her studies about the position of women in the changing world of Islam and through her critical feminist *relecture* of the origins of Islam.[3] For Fatema Mernissi, Islam is not a religiously and culturally mono-lithic edifice, but a broad spectrum of perspectives and points of view with which groups of people seek to explore the world and to find ways into a meaningful existence. At times these different points of view are at logger-heads with each other, at others – and this is the direction which F. Mernissi prefers – they in their diversity of expressions are close to each other. In her research and her literary writings F. Mernissi represents primarily the idea of the strong, intellectual and independent woman who at the same time is an integral part of the Islamic tradition. Such a woman cannot remain un-disputed following the views held in the West and the East, but according to F. Mernissi she has always played a predominant role in the Muslim world. In addition to the Qur'an and the *hadit*, i.e. the oral traditions about Muhammed, F. Mernissi gives high significance to the colourful traditional stories such as those collected in the 'Stories of Thousand and One Nights'. As a writer she finds herself mirrored in its fictional narrator, Sheherazade. Also the female presenters in the increasing number of Arabic news channels which are gaining increasing significance in society seem to represent in her view this mystical inventor of adventure stories.[4]

Arabic satellite channels like Al-Jazira and more recently Al-Arabia are increasingly becoming 24-hour news channels. Those who present this information are predominantly women; and the women who do this are 'not young and insecure' as is often the case on entertainment channels, but they show especially maturity with regard to age as well as to emotional balance, they have cerebral charisma and a confident appearance: it is this which men obviously find attractive. All of this has great cultural significance for F. Mernissi. She is convinced that first of all it weakens 'the stereotypes . . . which associate Islam with archaism'; and the fact that 'in the Arabic world it has become a national pass time to zap from one channel to the next' means that in future power has to be based in communication. The power shifts 'from the political and bureaucratic elite and from the particular interests of specific lobby groups within the oil producing industry to the citizens'. Second: with the communication required to do this one of the ancient ideals of Islam is realized: the *ummah*, the world-wide community of believers, is, according to F. Mernissi, not a static given, but a 'dynamic group, driven by communication' which has a tendency to cover the whole world. The Muslim dream 'of a planetary community linked through debates' which implies this, is, so she is convinced 'transformed into virtual reality' through the satellite channels. Third – and for F. Mernissi coming from a women's studies background, this is certainly not the least of the breakthroughs – the active and confident role of the presenters on the news channels implies the 'rejection of the archaic role of the dominant male whose masculinity is increased by the passivity of the woman'.

The relaxed and creative way in which F. Mernissi connects current questions with cultural and religious traditions, comes to the fore when she uses almost mystical language in speaking about the satellite channels. Like Sufi mysticism the news channels celebrate their manifold diversity through mirroring it. Diversity leads to confusion, and this generates fear, but precisely therein lies the mystical effect of satellite television: fear generates the desire to recognize that which causes fear, and to receive this with the help of the knowledge gained as personal gain for oneself. In an amusing way F. Mernissi inverts the received image of American culture as a culture which is open and oriented to the world and the Arabic one as closed: she associates America with the fearful behaviour of the cowboy who arms himself against and hides from strangers. In contrast she associates Arabic culture with the acts of Sindbad, the seafarer from the stories of a Thousand-and-One Nights who strays around the world, who always trades with strangers in a strange environment and has exchanges with them.[5] In a text which holds the balance between a story and an essay Mernissi explores the usefulness and the limitations of these two metaphors. She follows them where they are illuminating, and breaks them where they are in danger of confirming unfair stereotypes. She looks for the cowboys of the spirit in Arabic history – and locates the most significant ones not accidentally in Bagdad! She also researches what has led to the fact that in the Arabic tradition Sindbad has largely been replaced by the cowboy, and she tries to find ways and means to restore the honour of Sindbad-like behaviour in the Islamic world.

Even more than for F. Bernissi for Sadam Al-Azm (born in 1934 in Damascus) Islam is primarily more a cultural tradition to which he belongs than a religion. This second Erasmus-Laureate, Professor Emeritus for modern European philosophy, is a secularized and politically left-wing thinker who regards himself as a Muslim 'according to culture, heritage and history'. He endeavours to open up this tradition and to keep it that way. In this context he defended Salman Rushdie when his life was under threat from a fatwa by Ayatollah Khomeini for his novel *The Satanic Verses*.[6]

A month after 11 September 2001 Salman Rushdie wrote a column where he asked people to get used to the idea that the attacks certainly had to do with Islam. Thus Rushdie pleaded for Islam as a personal and privatized faith and argued for it 'depoliticization'. In an interview Al-Azm refers to an earlier essay by Rushdie where he points out that in the turbulent world in which we live it is impossible to withdraw to a quiet terrain outside of politics.[7] Hence Al-Azm is convinced that it is impossible to ban religion into the sphere of the private. Instead he tries to save Islam in its most sacred texts as a precious part of his own cultural heritage.[8] Here he prefers an ideally secularized context as his starting point.

In a polemical article he argues against the idea which has become popular in the current international debate, that Islam is not capable of secularization. First of all, such a statement is in contradiction to the facts. In fact, in Islamic countries like Egypt, Iraq, Syria, Algeria and Turkey religion has been pushed back to the margins of society. Especially the fact that Islam is moving towards 'privatization, personalization and even individualization' and that thus society is secularized, is according to Al-Azm the background of the violent reactions of radical Islamists. They aim for a re-Islamization of those societies which are now only Islamic societies in name.[9] Al-Azm summarizes his own answer to the question if Islam is capable of secularization as follows: 'From a dogmatic point of view Islam is not capable, from a historical perspective it is.' History in his opinion offers a clear proof that Islam is not the static dogmatic system which both those who agree with this thesis and those who oppose it are inclined to see in it. It is rather a 'living, dynamic, developing faith which is capable of adapting to very different environments and rapidly changing circumstances.' Religions develop continually along historical lines which to those who only have eyes for their own dogmatic system must appear to be nothing but impossible. Thus 'the simple, egalitarian and unpretentious Islam of Mecca and Medina' was, from a dogmatic point of view, incompatible with the might Kalifate which nevertheless would remain the classic form of government in the Arabic and Islamic world 'until Mustafa Kemal Atatürk officially abolished it'. Al-Azm finds an analogy in the Roman Catholic Church and the debate around the legacy of the Second Vatican Council. He names the 'movement of Archbishop Lefevre and his followers in Europe and the United States of America as an excellent example for the way in which the Church holds on to the purist dogmatic 'no' to the dominant paradigms of our time' and the Council with its documents as an 'equally fitting example as to how in the Roman Catholic

Church the historical 'yes' has overcome the classical 'no' [over against modernity].

Al-Azm is primarily a commentator on developments and trends in the intellectual life of the Muslim world. His own interest is in an Islamic culture which can once again play a role on the global stage. Thus he turns against the religious resistance 'against the modern system of scientific logic and the understanding of the world and the way we act in it', for this will end in 'surrendering to the dustbin of history'.[10] He is looking for a religious imagination which fits in with the modern world view and fosters democracy and openness to the insights of science. The particularity of Islam and the limitations which it sets to an authentic re-interpretation do not seem to interest him; he even seems to deny that such limitations exist.

The humanism of God

For all three Erasmus Laureates of 2004 it seems to be evident that religion is a human creation, a product of human imagination. In this sense all three of them have a humanist understanding of religion. In the case of the one who has not been mentioned yet, Hussein Dabbagh (born in 1945 in Teheran) who uses the nom de plum Abdulkarim Sourosh, this is carried by his belief in what the Flamish-Dutch Erasmus Laureate of 1982 Edward Schilebeeckx called the 'Humanism of God'.[11] In the eulogy Sourosh was called 'the Erasmus of Islam', and certainly among the three authors mentioned he is the one closest to the Dutch Christian humanist. Sourosh tries develop an alternative through thorough arguments as well as on the basis of contemporary philosophical insights into religion and science: on the one hand to secularism of the Western kind and on the other hand to religious dictatorship as it has taken shape in Iran, his country of origin. While he was a student in England, Sourosh was involved in the opposition against the Shah, and he returned to Iran after the Islamic Revolution in 1979. In 1980 he became a member of the Council for the Cultural Revolution set up by Ayatollah Khomeini. However, he left the latter in 1982 and has not held a government function since. He became a lecturer in Islamic mysticism at the University of Teheran and a member of the Iranian Academy of Science. Owing to the increasing criticism of Islamic clergy he lost his position and became subject to censorship and threats. In 1996 he left his country and has since taught in universities in the West.[12]

Sourosh rejects the idea that religion due to its inherent authoritarian

characteristics is incompatible with democracy. He takes up a detailed discussion with an article published in 1994 in the journal *Kiryan* with which he
has been involved since its founding. In this article Hamid Paydar argues:
'Islam and democracy cannot be combined with each other, unless Islam
were to be secularized through and through.'[13] Sourosh denies this, but not
– as would be the obvious strategy – by pointing out that in the Islamic legal
tradition there is room for open discussion and asking the opinion of the
people and hence for democratic consultation, but by pointing out that religion lives by faith. And faith is the personal answer given by each individual
on the basis of again and again renewed circumstances and is thus manifold
and pluralistic. Those who regard religions and Islam in particular as being
authoritarian and totalitarian as such wrongly identify them with their legal
and political traditions. In his view the 'constant renewal of insight' and the
'multiplicity of faith expressions' are an essential part of religion, which are
in the end of the day 'a thousand times more' compatible with democracy
than with secularism. In turn this means that the upholding of religious laws
as such rather kills religion than maintains its life and that at least an Islamic
legislation can only remain genuinely religious if it is an expression of a
religious community.

   As for Al-Azm it is of great importance for Sourosh that religion does not
exclusively live by its principles. It has to learn from the democratic and
rational attitudes which have been discovered and developed in modernity.
'Democracy is rooted in the new insight into itself and the limitations of
human knowledge which humanity has gained.' And if such thinking with
regard to human dignity, public rationality and the limitations of any form
of knowledge within religion are taken up, 'the result will be a religious
democracy'. The big difference to Al-Azm is however that for Sourosh even
such taking seriously of discoveries that do not immediately follow from
religion is not ultimately of religious significance. The search for truth and
justice, however not the setting of truth and justice, is the essence of
democracy.

   This according to Sourosh is also the essence of religion. Religion forbids
human beings to act as if they were God, and then what remains is the
rational debate 'about justice, human rights and the method of political
leadership' which according to Sourosh should not be regarded as something internal to religion. Religion in Sourosh's view is not a source of just
laws and rules of behaviour as many Muslims think. Religion according to
Sourosh takes care that the laws which to the best of their knowledge seek

to secure justice, human rights and administrative fairness, appear not as external restrictions of human freedom but as moral obligations. The religious superiority of democracy in his view not least originates from the fact that, while dictatorship and totalitarianism are deeply corrupt, democracy is most profoundly connected with moral, life-giving principles without which democracy is doomed.

In the face of his openness to democracy and modernity it seems at first glance surprising that Sourosh regards philosophy as the enemy of religion. His argument with regard to this is complicated but here he is explicitly concerned with Greek philosophy and the traditions that build on it. Greek philosophy orders the world in metaphysical categories. This gave the world and things their autonomy over against God, which makes rational thinking about it possible. However, at the same time it also reduces God's task for the future to the realization of previously noted essences of things. 'God was no longer creator of the essences but the one who took care that they would realize themselves.'

Thus according to Sourosh the things and ultimately God himself – who has become a mechanical cause among others – have been demythologized and removed from the world of religion. In a similar way, a juristic rationality which has been regarded as autonomous loses its religious significance, and even if it develops as an extension of a religious tradition. It takes the place of devout surrender which for Sourosh is the primary characteristic of religion, through submission of force exercised in the name of God. Ultimately Sourosh aims to allocate the rational balances of sciences, politics, government activity and law their place within the realm of religious faith which regards these balances in the shadow of God. It is not always obvious how he envisages this, but along with many philosophers and theologians in the West he is convinced that – speaking in his imagery – the veil which separates western thinking from religious thought is metaphysical thinking. For contemporary culture as well as for contemporary religion it is vital to tear away this mirror.

In the light of the current image of Islam Sourosh is held in high regard for hermeneutical understanding of religion which is not shaped by false concessions. 'It is for God to reveal a religion', he writes, 'but it is for us to understand it and to realize it. Here is the place where religious knowledge is born which is entirely human and subject to all rules of human knowledge.' The distinction which is so essential to all Islamic authors between the permanent which comes from God and that which can change and is thus culturally contingent, for him is in itself part of the process of acquiring knowledge and does not precede it. On the basis of this insight he seeks to come to a process of a basically endless process of religious revival and reform which in his eyes must involve social and political reform and permeate it.[14] Ultimately human life, even social and political life, in the eyes of Sourosh is a movement of religious search. In turn democracy is not a threat to religion rightly understood but to be precise its appropriate basis.

Fatema Mernissi and Sadik Al-Azm indicate that it is easily possible for a view to develop in the Islamic world which has a positive attitude to openness, democracy and pluralism. This is *inter alia* owed to the fact that Islam is not a privatized religion but also a wide-ranging cultural and political tradition. Here Al-Azm emphasizes that in today's world everything has political significance and that it would thus be an illusion to search for a quiet zone of pure non-political religion. Abdulkarim proves that it is possible to argue for an open, democratic Islam precisely on the basis of religion. Even in Islam the right is at home that God who is called upon as the merciful and compassionate, is a God deeply concerned with humanity, a *Deus humanissimus*.

Notes

1. M. Sparreboom, 'Religie en moderniteit. Inleiding' in *Religie en moderniteit: Fatema Mernissi, Sadik Al-Azm and Abdulkarim Sourosh*, Amsterdam, 2004, pp. 7–16; here p. 10. My article is to a large extent based on this collection of the three laureates' writings on the occasion of their being awarded the Erasmus Prize. This however has only been published in the Netherlands. Where texts are available in other languages, I refer to them in the notes.

2. Cf http://www.erasmusprijs.org/nl/page.cfm?paginalD-2

3. On the first topic see: F. Mernissi, *Dreams of Trespass: Tales from a Harem Girlhood*, Reading, 1994. On the second: *The Effects of Modernization of the Male-Female Dynamics in a Muslim Society: Marocco*, Diss., Ann Arbor 1974; later revised as: *Beyond the Veil: Male-Female Dynamics in Modern Muslim Society*, Cambridge, 1975, 21987 (revised edition) and *Le Maroc raconté par ses femmes*, Rabat, 1984. On the third topic: *Le harem politique: Le Problème et les femmes*, Paris, 1987.

4. 'The Satellite, the Prince, and Scheherazade: The Rise of Women as Communicators in Digital Islam' in *Transnational Broadcasting Studies* 12, (2004), http://www.tbsjournal.com/mernissi.htm.

5. 'De cowboy of Sinbad? Wie zal de winnaar zijn in de globalisering?' in *Religie en moderniteit*, ibid., pp. 17–55; this is a developed version of 'The Cowboy or Sinbad: Who Will Be the Globalization Winner?'

http://www.Fundacionprincipedeasturias.org/ing/premios/galardones/
galardonados/dicursos/discurso767.html.

6. On his relationship with Rushdie, see S. Al-Azm, 'The Satanic Verses Post Festum' in *Comparative Studies of South Asia, Africa and the Middle East* 20 (2000) Nr. 1–2, pp. 44–66.

7. 'An Interview with Sadik Al-Azm' in *Arab Studies Quarterly* 19 (1997), Nr. 3, pp. 113–126, here: p. 121; cf S. Rushdie, *Imaginary Homelands: Essays an Criticism 1981–1991*, London 1991, pp. 87–101: 'Outside the Whale (1984)', here: pp. 93–100.

8. 'An Interview with Sadik Al-Azm', ibid., p. 116.

9. S. Al-Azm, 'Is Islam Secularizable?' http://www.secularislam.org.separation/isislam.htm.

10. Quoted in S. Wild, 'Ten geleide' in Al-Azm, *De tragedie van de Duivel: Op weg naar een liberale islam*, Amsterdam, 2004, pp. 7–9, here p. 9.

11. Speech by Edward Schillebeeckx in *Praemium Erasmianum MCMIXXXLL*, Amsterdam, 1982, pp. 37–42, here p. 41.

12. V. Vakili, *Debating Religion and Politics in Iran: The Political Thought of Abdolkarim Soroush*, New York, 1997; M. Sadri/A. Sadri, 'Introduction' in eds. M. Sadri and A. Sadri, *S. Soroush, Reason, Freedom and Democracy in Islam: Essential Writings*, Oxford, 2000, pp. ix–xix; S. Sourosh, 'Intellectual Autobiography: An Interview', idem, pp. 3–25.

13. A. Soroush, 'Tolerance and Governance: A Discourse on Religion and Democracy' in *Reason, Freedom and Democracy in Islam*, ibid., pp. 131–155.

14. 'Islamic Revival and Reform: Theological Approaches' in S. Sourosh, *Reason, Freedom, and Democracy in Islam*, ibid., pp. 26–38, here p. 31 f.

III. Islam as Enlightening – Ongoing Dialogue

Islam: Radical Changes in History – Challenges of the Present

HANS KÜNG

Introduction

There is the threat of a *general suspicion* about – this time not against the Jews, but against Muslims: as if all of them, incited by their religion, are potentially violent. And as if in turn all Christians, taught by their religion, are non-violent, peaceful, and loving . . . That would be nice.

Let's be fair of course: we as citizens of a democratic state under the rule of law object in the name of human dignity to forced marriages, the oppression of women, honour killings and other archaic inhumanities. But so do, with us, most Muslims. They suffer if 'Muslims' or 'Islam ' as such are condemned. They do not find themselves in our image of Islam, because they want to be loyal citizens of Muslim religion.

Let's be fair: those who want to hold Islam responsible for the kidnappings, suicide attacks, car bombings and beheadings of some misguided extremists, ought also to condemn 'Christianity' or 'Judaism' for the barbaric abuse of prisoners, bombings and tank attacks (100,000 murdered civilians in Iraq alone) of the US Army and the terror of the Israeli occupying army in Palestine. Those who pretend that the fight for oil and hegemony in the Middle East and elsewhere is a 'struggle for democracy' and a 'war against terror' lies to the world – although without success.

The General Secretary of the UN Kofi Annan stressed in his Global Ethic lecture in 2003 in Tübingen: 'No religion and no ethical system should be condemned because of the moral derailments of some of its followers. If I as a Christian for example don't want my faith to be judged on the basis of the actions of the Crusaders or the Inquisition, I myself have to be very careful not to judge the faith of another on the basis of the actions which a small number of people commit in the name of their faith.'

Should we therefore continue to set off against each other which will only lead into deeper misery? No, what is required is a different basic attitude to violence and war, which basically all nations want, if they are not – as is the case in Arabic countries as well as in the USA – led astray by blinded rulers who are obsessed with power and stultified by ideologists and demagogues.

Violence has been exercised under the sign of the crescent but also under the sign of the cross, by medieval and contemporary 'crusaders' who have turned the cross from a sign of reconciliation into a sign of war. Both religions have throughout history expanded their spheres of influence aggressively and used violence to defend their power. In their realm they have propagated an ideology not of peace but of war. Thus the situation is complicated.

All of us are in danger of being completely drowned by the giant streams of information and thus to lose our sense of direction. And even religious studies scholars have been heard to voice the opinion that in their own discipline one can no longer see the wood for so many trees. And thus some – such as for example sociologists – concentrate on microstudies and are no longer willing or able to *think of the bigger picture*. Therefore new catagories are necessary to take into account the changes.

I am attempting to offer you a certain *basic orientation* about Islam in the context of the two other Abrahamic religions, Judaism and Christianity. Thus let us go straight into the topic. I want to discus three subject areas: I. The abiding centre and foundation: that which must be held on to; II. radical changes: that which can change; III. Contemporary challenges: the pressing task..

I. The abiding centre and foundation

What in our respective religions must be held on to, held on to at all costs? In all three prophetic religions we can find extreme positions: some say: 'There is nothing to hold on to'; others however say: 'We must hold on to everything.'

- There is 'nothing' to hold on to, say Christians who are *completely secularized*: they often believe neither in a God nor in a Son of God, they ignore the Church and go without sermons and sacraments . . .

At best they value the cultural heritage of Christianity: the cathedrals or Johann Sebastian Bach, the aesthetics of Orthodox liturgy or even paradoxically the Pope, whose sexual morality and authoritarianism they reject – of course – as a pillar of the established order.

–There is 'nothing' to hold on to, so say also completely *secularized Jews*: they disregard the God of Abraham and the patriarchs; they do not believe their promises, ignore synagogue prayers and rites and smile about the ultra orthodox.

For their kind of Judaism which is empty of religion they have often found a substitute religion: the state of Israel and the appeal to the Holocaust which even for secularized Jews creates at least a Jewish identity and solidarity, but which not infrequently also seems to justify the inhumane state terror against non-Jews.

–There is 'nothing' to hold on to, so say however also completely *secularized Muslims*: they do not believe in a God, they do not read the Qu'ran; for them Muhammad is not a prophet and they reject the sharia outright; the five pillars of Islam have no significance for them.

At best Islam, emptied of all religious significance, can be used as a tool for political Islamism, Arabism and nationalism.

It is understandable that as a counter-reaction to this 'hold on to nothing' the opposite call is heard: '*Hold on to everything*'. Everything should remain as it is and supposedly always was:

– 'no stone of the grand edifice of Catholic dogma must be removed, the whole thing would be shaken', thus trumpet *Roman Integralists*.

– 'No word of the Halacha must be neglected; behind every word is the will of the Lord (Adonai)', thus protest *ultra-orthodox Jews*.

– 'No verse from the Qu'ran must be ignored, each and every one of them is in the same way the immediate Word of God', thus insist many *Islamist Muslims*.

In all of these we find pre-programmed conflicts, not only *between* the three, but primarily *within the three religions* wherever these positions are held militantly or aggressively: the extreme positions frequently work each other up. 'Les extrêmes se touchent!'

However, the reality is not quite as bleak. For in most countries, unless they are charged up by political, economic, social factors, the extreme positions are not in the majority. There are still – dependent on the country and the time – a significant number of Jews, Christians and Muslims who – although themselves indifferent, complacent or ignorant in their religious practice – want to give up by no means everything in their Jewish, Christian or Muslim faith and life. On the other hand they want to retain by no means everything: as Catholics to swallow all the dogmas and moral teaching of Rome or as Protestants to accept each and every sentence in the Bible verbatim, or as Jews to keep everything in the Halacha, or as Muslims to keep strictly all commandments of the Sharia.

Whatever: if we look not at some of the later historical expressions and forms, but go back to the *original testimonies and testaments*, to the 'Holy Scriptures' of the respective religions – the Hebrew Bible, New Testament and Qu'ran – there can be no doubt that *what abides* (what must abide) in the respective religion is not simply identical with *what is* (what is at the present moment) and that that which forms the core, the substance, the essence of this particular religion, can be defined out of the 'Holy Scriptures' of the respective religion. What is at stake here is a very practical question: what in our religions, in our own religion, must be of *lasting validity and constant obligation*? We must *not hold on to everything*, but to the *substance of faith*, the centre and the foundation of the respective religion, of its Holy Scripture, its faith! Now for a concrete question however answered very briefly and in principle:

1. What must we hold on to in *Christianity* lest it should lose its 'soul'?

Answer: Whatever critical Biblical scholarship, historical, literary or sociological manages to critique, interpret or reduce: from the point of view of the important and historically significant testaments of faith, from the New Testament (read in the context of the Hebrew Bible) the central content of the faith is *Jesus Christ*: he as the Messiah and Son of the one God of Abraham, he, at work even today through the same *Spirit* of God. No Christian faith, no Christian religion without the confession: '*Jesus is the Messiah, Lord, Son of God!*' The name Jesus Christ marks the (by no means static) 'centre of the New Testament'.

2. What must we hold on to in *Judaism* lest it should lose its essence?

Answer: whatever a historical, literary or sociological critique may be able to critique, interpret and reduce: from the important and historically significant documents of faith, from the Hebrew Bible, the central content of the faith is the one *God* and the one *people of Israel*. No Israelite faith, no Hebrew Bible, no Jewish religion without the confession: '*JHWH (adonai) is the God of Israel, and Israel his people!*'

3. And finally, what must be held on to in *Islam*, if it wants to remain Islam in the actual sense of 'surrender', 'submission to God'?

Answer: however long and tedious the process of collecting, ordering and editing of the different chapters of the Qu'ran was, it is clear for all faithful

Muslims that the Qu'ran is the God's Word and Book. And even if Muslims do take into account the difference between the chapters from Mecca and those of Medina and regard the background of the revelation as a criterion for interpretation, the central message of the Qu'ran is very clear: '*There is no God but Allah, and Mohammed is his prophet.*'

Not the special relationship of the people of Israel with its God (as in Judaism), not even the special relationship of Jesus Christ with his God (as in Christianity), but the special relationship of the Qu'ran to God is the germinating seed and the constitutive focus of Islam. And in all the turmoil and confusion of the history of the Islamic nations this will remain the basic understanding of the Islamic religion which will not be surrendered.

To summarize: the *characteristics* of the three monotheistic religions *which must be retained* are at the same time something they share and something that separates them.

– What Judaism, Christianity and Islam *share*: the faith in the one and only God of Abraham, the gracious and merciful creator, sustainer and judge of all people.

– What *separates* them:

For Judaism: Israel as God's people and land.

For Christianity: Jesus Christ as the Messiah and Son of God.

For Islam: the Qu'ran as God's Word and Book.

In the constant centre of the three religion, Judaism, as is Christianity, as is finally Islam:

– *origins* since very early times,

– *continuity* in its long history through the centuries,

– *identity* in spite of differences between languages, peoples, cultures and nations.

Of course, this centre, this foundation, this substance of faith has never existed as a given in abstract isolation, has been interpreted and practically realized time and time again according to the changing demands of the times. And therefore the *systematic-theological and the historical-chronological representation*, without which the former cannot be justified convincingly, must *be combined*.

II. Epochal radical Changes

Time and time again *new epochal constellations* of the time – of society in general, of the community of faith, the proclamation of faith and reflection on it – will reinterpret and concretize this one centre. This history in Judaism, Christianity and Islam is incredibly dramatic: in response to new challenges in world history the community of small beginnings – though especially in the case of Christianity and Islam it grew very fast – has time and time undergone a number of fundamental religious transformations, in the long run even revolutionary *paradigm shifts*.

The theory of paradigms is only a hermeneutical framework, and only if it is carried out in a material-historical way and the present is analyzed will it show its full illuminating power. This I have shown in extensive studies of Christianity, Judaism and Islam, and on a more basic level also in searching for traces with regard to Hinduism, Buddhism and Chinese Religion. The strictly historical analysis of the paradigms of a religion, those *macro paradigms or epochal global constellations* serve the purpose of orienting knowledge. It offers the opportunity to carry out a selection for a global view of the history of religion as all encompassing as possible and yet also at the same time as precisely as possible. The analysis of paradigms makes possible the working out of the great historical structures and transformations: through concentrating at once on the fundamental *constants* as well as on the decisive *variables*. In this way we can outline those breaks in world history and the basic epochal models of a particular religion generated through them, which to this day determine their situation as patterns of perception.

On the background of such a considerable history we must attempt a historic-systematic analysis of its *global epochal constellation*. In my book *Christianity* I worked out the following macro paradigms in the history of *Christianity*:

1. the Jewish-apocalyptic paradigm of early Christianity;
2. the ecumenical-Hellenistic paradigm of Christian Antiquity;
3. the Roman Catholic paradigm of the Middle Ages;
4. the Protestant-Evangelical paradigm of the Reformation;
5. the modern paradigm of reason and progress;
6. the ecumenical paradigm of post-modernity?

In the same way, in *Judaism*, I have worked out the macro paradigms of *Judaism*:

1. the tribal paradigm of the pre-state time;
2. the kingdom paradigm of the monarchical time;

3. the theocratic paradigm of post-exilic Judaism;
4. the rabbinic-synagogal paradigm of the Middle Ages;
5. the paradigm of assimilation in modernity;
6. the ecumenical paradigm of post-modernity?

III. Contemporary Challenges

Thus each religion doers not appear as a static entity where supposedly everything has always been as it is today, but rather as a living developing reality which has gone through a number of different epochal constellations. Here the *first* decisive insight applies: paradigms can (with the exception of the very first) continue to exist well into the present! In contrast to the 'exact' *sciences*: there the old paradigm (such as that of Ptolemaeus) can be empirically verified or disproved; in the long run the decisions in favour of the new paradigm (of Copernicus) can be 'enforced' through evidence. In the realm of *religion* however (and also in the arts) this is different: with regard to questions of faith, of moral or rites nothing can be decided (for example between the East and the West of the Roman Empire or between Rome and Luther) in a mathematically exact way, and this in the context of religion the old paradigms by no means disappear as a matter of necessity. Rather they can *continue to exist* for centuries alongside new paradigms: the new paradigm (of the Reformation or of Modernity) alongside the old (that of the Early or the Medieval Church).

For the assessment of the situation of religions this persistence and competition of different paradigms is of the utmost importance. A *second* important insight: Why? To this day *followers of the same religion live in different paradig*ms! They are formed by abiding basic principles and subject to certain social mechanisms. Within Christianity for example there are even today *Roman Catholics* who live intellectually in the thirteenth century (alongside Thomas Aquinas, the Medieval Papacy and the absolutist church order). There are some representatives of *Eastern Orthodoxy* who are intellectually stuck in the fourth and fifth century (alongside the Greek Fathers of the Church). And for some Protestants the pre-Copernican constellation of the sixteenth century (with the pre-Copernican Reformers, prior to Darwin) is still authoritative.

In a similar way some Arabs still dream of the great Arab Empire and long for all Arab peoples to be united into one Arab nation ('Pan-Arabism'). Others do not regard being Arab but Islam as that which links the nations and prefer a 'Pan-Islamism'. Some orthodox Jews regard medieval Judaism as their ideal and reject the modern state of Israel. In turn many Zionists aim for a state within the borders of the Davidic–Solomonic Empire.

It is especially this continuation, this persistence and competition of previous religious paradigms today which must be one of the main causes of conflict within religions and between them, the main cause for different traditions and parties, of tensions, conflicts and wars. As a *third* important insight we can identify: for Judaism as well as for Christianity and for Islam the central question is: how does this religion relate to its own *Middle Ages* (which at least in Christianity and in Islam are regarded as the 'time of greatness') and how do they relate to *Modernity* where all three religions regard themselves as cornered into the defensive. Christianity had to undergo after the Reformation a further paradigm shift, that of the Enlightenment. Judaism in contrast went through the Enlightenment first and then, at least in its Reform tradition, experienced a religious reformation. Islam however did not go through a religious reformation and therefore to this day also struggles with Modernity.

Many Jews, Christians and Muslims who agree with the modern paradigm, get on better with each other than with their own fellow believers who live in different paradigms. In turn Roman Catholics who are stuck in the Middle Ages might be able to join forces with regard to questions of sexual morality with the 'Medieval' within Islam and within Judaism (UN Conference on World Population Cairo 1994).

Those who want *reconciliation* and peace will not be able to avoid a critical analysis of paradigms. Only thus we can answer questions like: where in the history of Christianity (and of course in other religions) are the constants and variables, where are continuity and discontinuity, where is agreement and where resistance? This is a *fourth* insight: what we must hold on to is mainly the essence, the foundations, the core of a religion and the constants which are given in its origin. What we must not necessarily hold on to are those things which are not essential in their origin, those things that are husk and not core, extension and not foundation. We can surrender (or in turn develop) the different variables when this appears necessary.

Thus an analysis of the paradigms is in the light of all the religious confusion especially *in the age of globalization* in aid of *global orientation*. We are without a doubt in a critical key phase of reshaping international relationships, of the relationship between the West and Islam and the relationships between the three Abrahamic religions Judaism, Christianity and Islam.

The options have become evident: either rivalry between the religions, clash of cultures, war of the nations – or *dialogue of cultures and peace between the religions as a prerogative for peace between the nations*! Shouldn't we in the face of the threat of the destruction of humanity as a whole stop building bulwarks of hatred, of retaliation and enmity and rather tear down the walls of prejudice brick by brick in order to use them to build bridges of dialogue, bridges especially towards Islam?

IV. Islam and global ethic

For the building of these bridges it is crucial: as different as the three religions are, and as different again the different paradigms which change over the centuries and millennia: there are, especially on the level of ethics, constants which make the building of such bridges possible.

Since human beings developed out of the animal kingdom and became human, they also learnt to behave in a humane and not in an inhuman way. As human beings are by nature ruled by their instinctive urges in spite of their now developed ability to use reason the beast has remained a reality within humanity. And again and again human beings have to make the effort to act in a humane and not an inhuman way.

Thus we find in all religious, philosophical and ideological traditions some simple ethical imperatives of humanity which to this day are of the greatest significance:

  – 'no murder – but also no torture, torment or violence' – or positively: 'Respect for life'. The commitment to a culture of *non-violence* and *respect for all life*.
  – 'no stealing – but also no exploitation, bribery, corruption' or positively: 'Act with honesty and fairness.' The commitment to a culture of *solidarity* and a *just economic order*.
  – 'no lying – but also no deceit, forgery, manipulation', or positively: 'speak and act truthfully!' The commitment to a culture of *tolerance* and a *truthful life*.
  – and finally: 'no abuse of sexuality – but no abuse of the partner at all, no denigration or humiliation', or positively: 'respect and love one another!' The commitment to a culture of *equality* and the *partnership of men and women*.

These four ethical imperatives can be found in the work of Patanjali, the founder of Yoga, as well as in the Buddhist canon, the Hebrew Bible as well as in the New Testament and also in the Qu'ran. They are based on two basic ethical principles:

– first, there is the *Golden Rule*. It was formulated already by Confucius, many centuries before Christ and is known in all great religious and philosophical traditions but can by no means be taken for granted: 'Do not do to others what you do not wish for yourself.' As basic as this rule is, as helpful is it in some difficult situations.

– the Golden Rule is supported by the *Rule of Humanity* which is by no means tautological: 'Every human being – whether young or old, man or woman, disabled or able-bodied, Christian, Jew or Muslim – must be treated humanely and not inhumanely.' Humanity, the human, is indivisible!

From all this it is evident that the shared human or global ethic is not an ethical system like that of Aristotle, Thomas Aquinas or Kant ('ethics') but some basic ethical values, rules and attitudes which should form the personal moral convictions of the human person and society (ethic).

This ethic is of course always contra-factual: the imperatives of humanity are not fulfilled *a priori*, but have to called to mind and realized time and time again. As Kofi Annan said in his Global Ethic lecture in Tübingen in 2003: 'If it is wrong to condemn a particular faith or a particular value system on the basis of the actions or statements of its followers, then it must be equally wrong to give up the idea that certain values are *universal*, only because there are some who do not appear to accept these values.'

Let me therefore conclude with the same words with which the General Secretary of the United Nations closed his lecture: 'Are there still universal values? Yes, there are, but we must not take them for granted. They must be carefully thought through, they must be defended, and they must be strengthened.

And we must find in ourselves the will to live by the values which we proclaim – in our private lives, in our local and national commonwealth and in the world.'

Translated by Natalie K. Watson

Does the Concept of 'Abrahamic Religions' have a Future?

In recent history of encounters between Christians and Muslims the concept of 'Abrahamic religions' is sometimes used as a 'summary' term. In this article I want to show that this term does more justice to the self understanding of Judaism, Christianity and Islam than terminology from a religious studies background. At the same time a closer analysis shows that reference to Abraham raises a number of problems. Two of these I want to discuss here: the fact that the Abraham narratives also contain a number of rather violent aspects; and the fact that 'Abraham' always has a function within a particular context into which some are included and others excluded. Regardless my final conclusion will be that there is a future for the concept 'Abrahamic religions' if it instructs us that for Jews, Christians and Muslims the narratives around Abraham and their interpretations in the three religions raise the issue of the mutual construction of negative images. I argue for the construction of an 'Abrahamic house of teaching' which also has an eye for the ambiguity which is inherent in each religion.

I. The reference to Abraham as the common ancestor

Until some decades ago common features between Judaism, Christianity and Islam were referred to primarily with the help of a terminology which had been taken from phenomenology. Following more descriptive adjectives such as 'Semitic' and 'West-Asian' one primarily used terms such as 'monotheistic religions', 'prophetic religions; and 'religions of the book'. These terms however merely identify similarities with regard to the central elements of these religions and thereby remain on the level of formal characterization. The term 'Abrahamic religions' however offers two obvious advantages in this regard. First of all, the term implies a reference to history which points to the fact that Judaism, Christianity and Islam share a common history which distinguishes them from other monotheistic religion such as Zoroastrianism. Secondly, the term links the reference to God in these religions with precisely these concrete historic events: here is a God who called Abraham to begin something new. While the Hebrew Bible emphasizes the leaving of land and family and the journey to a new country (Genesis 12.1), the Qur'an regard Ibrahim as the model righteous believer who is led by God on the right path (16.120–1).

On the basis of the reference to this shared history the concept of 'Abrahamic religions' first of all identifies that the religions are related to each other. This kinship has a biological dimension which is why Jewish believers often emphasize Abraham as their ancestor with reference to their being descended from his son Isaac while many Muslims regard him as their ancestor through his oldest son Ishmael. At the same time this kinship also has a spiritual dimension, which is primarily emphasized by Christians and Muslims if they speak of Abraham as the believer as such. It is this reference to the faith of Abraham which in my opinion is decisive for the use of his name in the dialogue between Christians and Muslims today.[1] I will return to this later.

Because of this reference to a shared history which primarily emphasizes the spiritual kinship of believers with Abraham the term 'Abrahamic religions' seems to have a great future in inter-religious dialogue. Karl-Josef Kuschel, Leonard Swidler and Bruce Feiler refer to a number of initiatives which are linked to the name of Abraham.[2] At the same time historic studies also show that the three religions in their relationships throughout history have associated a number of divergent and even polemical interpretation with Abraham. The relationships between the three religions are marked through interpretations which are likely to lead to conflict. They use the shared origin to mark one's own identity and thus to reject the claims of the others, just like children with regard to their parents' legacy who were neither Jew nor Christian but a *hanîf* and a Muslim (3.67). These words only want to say that Abraham venerated te one true God and submitted to him but the idea that Abraham was the prototype of an Islamite in the contemporary sense of the word is not far off for many Muslims. Even more polemical is according to the Gospel of John the argument between Jesus and 'the Jews' about the question who were the true descendents of Abraham. Here Jesus declares himself to be the prototype: 'Before Abraham was, I am.' (John 8.58).[3]

When John of Damascus around the year 730 as a monk in the monastery of Mar Sabbas wrote his main theological word *Source of Knowledge*, he included in it a description of a new religion about which he had learnt in his youth at the court of the Umayyads. In a list of the heresies he lists this religion as follows: 'There is also the (erroneous) faith of the Ishmaelites which dominates unto this day and as a precursor of the anti-Christ is the deceiver of humanity. It goes back to Ishmael, the son of Abraham and Hagar, and thus the followers of this faith are called 'Hagarenes' and 'Ishmaelites'. They are also called 'Saracenes' which is derived from 'sent away by Sarah with empty hands'. This is because of the words of Hagar to the angel: "Sarah sent me away empty handed."' Almost each one of the words in this sentence can be interpreted polemically as a reference to the injustice of the rule of Islamic authorities over Christians. In this way these words were read historically by Christians as John of Damascus was significant for the Christian reaction to Islam.[4] The polemical reaction however insinuates an Islamic self identification with descent from Abraham through Hagar and Ishmael: the Christian theologian speaks in the form of diatribes which correspond with being called names on the part of Muslims. This insinuates a common framework of understanding with Abraham and Christ.[5] John of Damascus treats the orthodox faith in Christ as the norm and thus is able to come to the conclusion that this new religion is not up to the norm as the Qur'an mentions Jesus with reverence but denies his divine origin. Others are more careful in applying such a norm. Thus Patriarch Timotheos I, in his famous dialogue with Kalif al-Mahdi (about 780), speaks of a precious pearl which lost in a house full of people. Everyone who begins to search for it in the dark will think that they have found a pearl, but as soon as it is light, it will be evident who has found a stone or a piece of clay and who the real pearl. This narrative in turn is reminiscent of the parable of the three rings in Boccaccio or Lessing where each of the three sons receives a ring, but only one of the three rings is the genuine one.[6] Time and time again the three religions are described in the image of three relatives who each claim to be the genuine heir. In most cases each one thinks that they already have the truth which can lead to the aforementioned polemics and unfortunately also to more serious forms of violence. Sometimes however there is a kind of eschatological reserve, and there is the awareness that God alone knows the truth and will reveal it at the end of time. Quite rightly Karl-Josef Kuschel links his interpretation of Lessing's parable with the request in the Qur'an to compete with each other with good deeds.[7] Here we begin to see a form of pluralism which links the diversity of religions with God's commandment to learn from the differences. If Abraham's heirs can bear this eschatological deferral of truth claims, then the reference to Abraham has a chance to survive the contemporary situation of sharpening contrasts and violence justified through religion.

II. Faith and violence in the narratives around Abraham

The previous section concluded with a beautiful vision. Those who make the effort to study the narratives around Abraham in more depth can do no other than be terrified about the violence which we encounter there, and particularly the religious justifications for this violence. The first example which catches the eye of the religiously aware reader is the narrative known in the Jewish tradition as the 'binding' of Isaac (*akedat Jitzhak*). In the Christian tradition one refers to 'sacrifice' instead of 'binding', probably because of the ancient association with the sacrifice of the other beloved son, Jesus Christ. Reuven Firestone and more recently Yvonne Sherwood have shown that the traditions of Islam also know numerous traditions about such attempted sacrifices, and that there we can find contradictory attitudes to the willingness to sacrifice expected by the people acting in the stories.[8] It is however a relief that it is the attitude of faith which in the Christian and Islamic tradition is linked especially with Abraham and his son which leads to the willingness to sacrifice and to be sacrificed. The Qur'an relates the dialogue between father and son as follows: "'O son! I truly saw in my vision that I sacrificed you; now what is your view?" He said: "O father! Do as you are bidden; you will find me by the Will of God steadfast."'[9] Their attitude is described in the Qur'an as an attitude of submission to God: *aslamâ*, they 'offered Islam'. Dutch readers will inevitably think of the title of the film *Submission*, made by Ayaan Hirsi Ali and Theo van Gogh to express their disgust about the treatment of women in the world of Islam. They will also think of how Mohammed B. justified his supposed obligation to slaughter Theo van Gogh (*dhabaha*, the same word which is used in the above verse from the Qur'an and which also had a central place in the documents found which related to the suicide assassins of 11 September 2001).[10] The *in sha' Allah* of the gentle boy in the Qur'an (37.102) finds its echo in the words of the Son, distressed to death, in Matthew 26.39: 'Father, if it is possible, let this cup pass me by! But not my will but yours be done.' A long tradition of Theodicee says of course that in the end of the day there was no sacrifice and the God's request was merely a test for Abraham. But of course it remains true that what is introduced here is a form of submission to God which is obviously at the expense of human relationships.

This conclusion shows at least that we cannot easily equate the kind of faith which is at the centre of the Abraham narratives with forms of faith which are the focus of later Abrahamic traditions. If Abraham really existed his faith was probably a form of lay spirituality for which family ties were the primary context for the development of his personal relationship with God.[11] Part of this is also the care for the continued existence of the family in changed cultural situations. This could be a possible explanation why Abraham can speak, apparently without a problem, about his wife as his sister and allows her to led into the harem of Pharaoh (Genesis 12.15) and of Abimelech (Genesis 20.2) Along the same lines is the reading of the Womanist theologian Delores Williams of the story of Hagar's survival in the desert as a story which makes a new future possible.[12] The feminist interpretation of the same story by Phyllis Trible however does not share the same optimism, primarily because God is obviously on the side of the oppressed. Phyllis Trible points to the same text as John of Damascus where Hagar complains to the angel, but the angel cautions her and tells her to return to her mistress and to obey her (Genesis 16.9). It gets even worse when Hagar calls upon God as *El-roï*, the God who sees me, because God comes to help her. Even stronger: God hears only the boy, although it was Hagar who called (Genesis 21.17), and thus the narrator uses his expertise to make the woman vanish from the story, in order to be able to concentrate on the male heir.[13] Each dialogue between religions today which pays attention to Abraham, Isaac and Jacob, but not to Sarah and Hagar, is in a sense a repetition of this patriarchal manoeuvre.

The concentration on the male heirs which may have played a central role in the original Abraham narratives leads to a number of different forms of sexual violence in these stories. Together with the religious justification of the willingness to sacrifice and to be sacrificed, these forms of sexual violence obviously ask for a form of censorship which declare these texts as only suitable for very grown-up specialists. However, I want to plead for putting these narratives in inter-textual connection with the history of their interpretation within the three Abrahamic religions in an Abrahamic house of teaching, for the simple reason that they are obviously religious classics in the sense in which David Tracy has written about them.[14] They all contain high ideals to which the religions are indebted for what makes them attractive, but also all manner of violence and terror with which religions are so frequently associated these days, primarily of course Islam. The narratives are not as ambiguous as religions are, and the advantage of that is it is possible in inter-religious dialogue the negative sides too, possibly in the first instance the negative sides of the images which Jews, Christians and Muslims have created of each other. With Hugh Goddard I plead to discuss the negative sides of our image of the other publicly, so that the negative sides of our own religions become visible too.[15] This of course requires a sphere of security which can only be generated if we within the 'Abrahamic house of teaching' learn from each other together and with patience from the classic texts which we have received from our respective traditions.

III. The context of a symbol: Louis Massignon and the faith of Abraham

In the preceding section I have shown that reference to Abraham serves largely as a symbol for the agreements between Jews, Christians and Muslims, although they often appear coupled with forms of violence between the religions which in a sense reflect the violence in the Abraham narratives themselves. Like every symbol 'Abraham' has his place in a network of contextual interpretations which allow the symbol to function better in some situations than in others. So the Israeli scholar Alon Goshen-Gottstein argued on the occasion of a conference on religion and peace in the light of the common ancestor Abraham held in Turkey that this reference seems to work primarily in the relationship between Muslims and Christians while the Jews tend to watch from the margins.[16] I think that Goshen-Gottstein touches a sore point here: this is about a theological symbolization which goes along better with the Islamic and Christian view on Abraham than with the Jewish perspective.

As Goshen-Gottstein explains himself, the modern use of Abraham probably began with the French Islamologist Louis Massignon (1883 – 1962) who spoke of Islam as a revival of the Abrahamic faith.[17] It is no exaggeration that Massignon spent all his life being fascinated with the figure of Abraham. Particularly his 'Trois prières d'Abraham, père de tous les croyants' are still a source of inspiration for the dialogue between Muslims and Christians.[18] Massignon however offers a very spiritual interpretation of Abraham which is not devoid of what we nowadays call Orientalism.[19] Along the lines of Massignon the Second Vatican Council in two very important texts links the faith of Abraham with the faith of Muslims. In *Lumen Gentium* 16 the Council speaks of 'Muslims who, professing to hold the faith of Abraham, along with us adore the one and merciful God, who on the last day will judge mankind.'[20] Even more explicitly this link is made in *Nostra Aetate* 3: 'they take pains to submit wholeheartedly to even His inscrutable decrees, just as Abraham, with whom the faith of Islam takes pleasure in linking itself, submitted to God.'[21] Although both texts speak at greater length about Jews than about Muslims, Abraham is particularly connected with the faith of the Muslims. The connection which Muslims themselves make is recognized here. The verb 'to submit' (Latin: se submittere) evokes by itself the idea of the Arabic equivalent *aslamâ* and thereby obviously confirms the Qur'anic claim that Abraham was a Muslim. It is clearly evident that the focus here is meant to be on a spiritual kinship with Abraham as the model believer, a kinship which connects Muslims and Christians with each other while the biological kinship of Muslims with Abraham (through Ishmael) is carefully circumnavigated.[22] Thus a net of different meanings is cast, which connects with Pauline argumentations, where the *faith* of Abraham – in contrast to relying on the *law* – is given a central role (Romans 4 and Galatians 3). In this network of meanings Jews only play a negative role as they are through the emphasis which they place on descent 'according to the flesh' the antipodes of this faith.

I thus come to the conclusion that the use of Abraham as a symbol for naming the common features in inter-religious dialogue is always defined by the contexts and thus includes some while it excludes others. In the example referred to above the Jews are the excluded party; sometimes however Muslims may be excluded on the basis of a shared use of the symbol through Jews and Christians.[23] In this regard it seems evident to me that the calling upon the name of Abraham in the dialogue between the two religions almost inevitably implies that this also has an effect on the third religion. I myself have often seen it in dialogues between Christians and Muslims what a healing effect the intervention of Jews can be, although it is often regarded as a nuisance.[24] In any case the symbol 'Abraham' serves to point out to the religions that their dialogue must never degenerate into a convivial get together, in which the existing relationships of power are left untouched.[25]

Ultimately, God asks Abraham to move away from what is and to begin something new. Ultimately the Abraham symbol itself must be opened up, in order to include in it those religions and world views, which are not part of the network of interpretations, but are nevertheless linked with his name.

The first step however seems to me to be for the time being the building of a new generation which will then have learnt with the help of an Abrahamic teaching house to grapple with the ambiguity of their religions and to work on their mutual concepts of their enemies. In this context the reference to Abraham will retain its significance.

*Translated by Natalie K. Watson on the basis of the
German translation by Ansgar Ahlbeck.*

Notes

1. Cf Karl-Josef Kuschel, *Streit um Abraham. Was Juden, Christen und Muslime trennt – und was sie eint*, Munich/Zurich, 1994; Bruce Feiler, *Abraham: A Journey to the Heart of Three Faiths*, New York, 2002.

2. Karl-Josef Kuschel, 'Op weg naar een Abrahamitische spiritualiteit en oecumene' in Pim Valkenberg/Ertürk Alasag/Greco Idema/Janneke Teunissen/ Carla Robertson (eds), *In de voetsporen van Abraham*, Budel, 2004, pp. 89–96; Leonard Swidler, 'Islam and the Trialogue of Abrahamic Religions' *Cross Currents* 42 (1992), pp. 444 – 452; Bruce Feiler, *Abraham*, pp. 221–226.

3. Cf Sjef van Tilborg, 'Jezus tenmidden van de Joden van het loofhuttenfeest in Johannes 8' in Henk J.M. Schoot (ed.), *Theologie en Exegese. Jaarboek 2001*, Thomas Instituut te Utrecht, Utrecht, 2002.

4. Norman Daniel, *Islam and the West: The Making of an Image*, Oxford, 1993 (1. edition Edinburgh, 1960), p. 13.

5. For more details see Adelbert Davids and Pim Valkenberg, 'John of Damascus: The Heresy of the Ismaelites' in Barbara Roggema/Marcel Poorthuis/Pim Valkenberg (eds), *The Three Rings. Textual Studies in the Historical Trialogue of Judaism, Christianity, and Islam*, Leuven, 2005, pp. 71–90.

6. See the introduction to the final chapter of *The Three Rings* (for details see previous note).

7. Karl-Josef Kuschel, *Vom Streit zum Wettstreit der Religionen: Lessing und die Herausforderung des Islam*, Düsseldorf 1998. Cf Pim Valkenberg, 'The Future of Religion: From Interreligious Dialogue to Multiple Identity?' in *Studies in Interreligious Dialogue* 14 (2004), pp. 95–107; here p.104.

8. Reuven Firestone, *Journeys in Holy Lands: The Evolution of Abraham-Ishmael Legends in Islamic Exegesis*, Albany, 1990; Yvonne Sherwood, '*Binding-Unbinding*: Divided Responses of Judaism, Christianity and Islam to the "Sacrifice" of Abraham's Beloved Son' *Journal of the American Academy of Religion* 72 (2004), pp. 821–861.

9. Qur'an 37. 102. English translation from *The Koran. Translation* Translated by S.V. Mir Ahmed Ali. Elmhurst, NY, 2004.

10. Cf Sherwood, loc. cit., pp. 823–824.

11. Kees Waaijman, *Spiritualiteit: vormen – grondslagen – methoden*, Kampen/ Gent, 2000, pp. 23–24.

12. Delores Williams, 'Hagar's Story: A Route to Black Women's Issues' in *Sisters in Wilderness: the Challenge of Womanist God-Talk*, Maryknoll, 1994, pp. 15–33.

13. Phyllis Trible, *Texts of Terror: Literary-Feminist Readings of Biblical Narratives*, Philadelphia, 1984.

14. David Tracy, *The Analogical Imagination: Christian Theology and the Culture of Pluralism*, London 1981.

15. Hugh Goddard, *Christians and Muslims: From Double Standards to Mutual Understanding*, Richmond, 1995, p.9.

16. Alon Goshen-Gottstein, 'Abraham and "Abrahamic Religions" in Contemporary Interreligious Discourse: Reflections of an Implicated Jewish Bystander', *Studies in Interreligious Dialogue* 12 (2002), pp. 165–83.

17. Cf Sidney Griffith, 'Sharing the Faith of Abraham: the "Credo" of Louis Massignon', *Islam and Christian-Muslim Relations* 8 (1997), pp. 193–210.

18. Louis Massignon, *Parole donnée*, Paris, 1962; G. Basetti-Sani, *Louis Massignon: Christian Ecumenist, Prophet of Interreligious Reconciliation*, Chicago, 1974; Guy Harpigny, *Islam et Christianisme selon Louis Massignon*, Louvain-la-Neuve, 1981.

19. Edward Said thus refers to Massignon as one of the first modern Orientalists: *Orientalism: Western Conceptions of the Orient*, London, 1978, pp. 263ff

20. http://www.vatican.va/archive/hist_councils/ii_vatican_council/documents/vat-ii_const_19641121_lumen-gentium_en.html.

21. http://www.vatican.va/archive/hist_councils/ii_vatican_council/documents/vat-ii_decl_19651028_nostra-aetate_en.html.

22. See Georges Anawati's commentary on *Nostra Aetate* 3 in *Lexikon für Theologie und Kirche*, second edition, volume XIII, Freiburg 1967, p. 486.

23. Cf for example Tarek Mitri, 'The Abrahamic Heritage and Interreligious Dialogue: Ambiguities and Promises', *Current Dialogue* 36 (December 2000), pp. 20–23.

24. With regard to content I am primarily thinking about the important significance of the emphasis on the differences between the religions. Cf for example Jonathan Sacks, *The Dignity of Difference: How to Avoid the Clash of Civilizations*, London 2002, but also Jonathan Magonet, *Talking to the Other: Jewish Interfaith Dialogue with Christians and Muslims*, London 2003.

25. This is quite rightly pointed out by the South African liberation theologian Farid Esack, *Qur'an, Liberation and Pluralism: an Islamic Perspective of Interreligious Solidarity Against Oppression*, Oxford, 1997, p. 258.

The Transcendent and Present God as Space of Enlightenment: The Theological Dialogue between Christians and Muslims as a Contribution to Modernity

ERIK BORGMAN

Amongst other things this issue of *Concilium* wants to show that Islam is not the clear-cut political and religious system which its opponents as well as its followers so frequently envisage. If we start from such a view, such a representation of religion as a complex of fixed persuasions about statistical truths, then we can only regard those who think differently as infidels or apostates. Ultimately this can lead to others being denied the right to life itself. Thus the insight is important that the Islamic tradition – like any other religious tradition – is a conglomerate of views, ways of thinking and discussions about human existence, the right ordering of such existence and its relationship with God as transcendent reality.

The question at the end of this issue is: what does this mean for Christian-theological interaction with Islam? How should theologians approach Islam? There are two sub-sets to this question: first of all the question as to how we should study Islam. The reply presented in this issue is: not as a static entity, as a fixed conviction, as a faith resting on an unchangeable holy book, but as a dynamic, living and thus developing tradition, which in interaction with the given situation takes concrete shape.[1] To take Islam seriously should mean for everyone, but especially for theologians, to take Islam seriously *as a religion*. This implies not regarding Islam as an autonomous and closed entity but as a world view which aims to encounter God in his dealing with the world as its creator and merciful guardian and to present him as such. This means that for the study of Islam it will not suffice to take a religious studies point of view where religion can be described and understood from the outside. We equally need a theological attitude which does not look *at* a religion, but considers it *together* with its religious tradition. In concrete terms, with regard to Islam we need to articulate what the world looks like with Islamic eyes 'with regard to God', 'from God's point of view', in order then to be able to assess the plausibility and the profitability of such an approach.[2] We will not do justice to Islam if we regard it as a collection of strange and arbitrary convictions but only if we view it as a form of life before God, in thankful submission under the will of God with God's judgement before our eyes.[3]

In this way Islam and Christianity amongst the other religions and world views become of themselves dialogue partners who can learn from each other to see things which they would not have seen by themselves and to make statements which they would not have made themselves. This leads us to the second sub-set of the question about the right approach to Islam: how should theology enter the dialogue with Islam? This sub-question is the subject of this concluding article.

In order to answer it, I want to take as my starting point a quotation from the Second Vatican Council's Declaration on Religious Freedom:

> Truth, however, is to be sought after in a manner proper to the dignity of the human person and his social nature. The inquiry is to be free, carried on with the aid of teaching or instruction, communication and dialogue, in the course of which men explain to one another the truth they have discovered, or think they have discovered, in order thus to assist one another in the quest for truth.[4]

It is important that the declaration *Dignitatis humanae* does not justify religious freedom with the help of the liberal idea of a freedom of choice which is in principle unrestricted. It rather starts with the thesis that the obligation to obey the truth requires individual and collective freedom. This freedom even involves – and it is not insignificant to emphasize this in the context with the current anti-Muslim attitudes in many Western countries – the freedom of the religions, 'to show the special value of their doctrine in what concerns the organization of society and the inspiration of the whole of human activity'.[5] Everyone has to be free on the basis of arguments to argue for example that it would mean a qualitative improvement for society if homosexuality was banned or if men go swimming separately from women, in the same way that everyone should be free to present the opposite. This is important not because the respective statement might be true, but so that their confirmation or rejection might become possible in the process of searching the truth and so that at the same time those insights of truth can be retained which might be hidden in the thesis which is to be contradicted. To say it in the language of *Dignitatis humanae*: in order to help one another in the search for truth.

When the question is asked if Muslims and Christians have the same God, what is meant most of the time is: to what extent do the images of God emerging from the respective traditions agree with each other? However, in continuation with *Dignitatis humanae* Christians and Muslims do have the same God as they are *searching* for the same God. And as Christians and Muslims, as do by the way Jews, seek the face of the God of heaven and earth, their God must of necessity also be the same: by definition there is only one such God.[6] Muslims and Christians meet each other in their discussions because they seek the true God and not on the basis of a common origin. Thus they can make an important contribution to modern culture. This is at least the thesis of this article.

'What do you stand for?' or 'Before what do you bend your knees?'

The journal *Concilium* stands for a tradition in which modernity and the Christian faith are not seen as being in contradiction with each other. Critical reason and human freedom are not in contradiction to the Christian tradition but to some extent they flow from this tradition; they are thus a concrete realization of this tradition. As much as I share this view, there is however an essential difference between a religious world view and the place of human beings in this world on the one hand and the conventional modern way of looking at this on the other hand. As a consequence religious faith to modern eyes frequently appears to be 'outdated' – and that Islam represents an 'outdated culture' is a position which the populist politician Pim Fortuyn proclaimed in the Netherlands and which after his death has shaped public opinion about religion in general and about Islam in particular.

The essential difference between the modern and the religious understanding of humanity appears most clearly in the modern emphasis of human autonomy and independence in contrast to the religious emphasis of submission and obedience. It is not surprising that particularly in this respect Islam is a stumbling block for it is Islam in particular which strongly emphasizes obedience and submission to a sovereign God. 'Islam' according to the conventional etymology means 'handing over'. In contrast the central question of modernity to human beings is: 'What do you stand for?' while the central religious question is: 'To what do you bow?'

This difference of opinion about that which makes the life of human beings valuable and what human beings can achieve or receive is connected with yet another even more significant difference. If we can imagine that life might *have meaning*, then the reality in which we live has indeed to appear as an instance which can indeed *give meaning* to life. This idea in particular is extremely problematic in modernity. In the modern world view it is a starting point which is taken for granted that the world receives meaning and significance through human beings giving such meaning and such significance to it. The world, history and the life of the individual are as such only regarded as chaos, arbitrary and void, and they only receive meaning by human beings giving it to it. Meaning and significance according to modern conviction do not emerge from the world but from the human world *view*. World views and religion thus appear automatically as forms of giving meaning, as an expression of convictions. From a religious point of view however human life is not meaningful because human beings *give* meaning to the world, but because this meaning is *received* from God or the gods, from a mystery which is hidden in and behind things, from a divine revelation in a text which is regarded as sacred.[7]

Believers can lay great emphasis on autonomy. They can – and in my view Christians must even do this – see in their autonomy the fulfillment of human life and in freedom expression and sign of the fact that human beings are the image of God. But while according to the liberal view everyone has a free choice as long as there is nothing put in the way of this natural freedom, autonomy and freedom are not to be taken granted in the awareness of believers or a product of their own efforts but a gift from above. In addition to that, it is a gift which human beings owe to each other. It is our task to give each other autonomy and freedom as they have also been given to us. In a typically religious paradox we are tied in out freedom and even our autonomy is not autonomous.

There is however also a religious variant of the modern scheme of thought according to which religions are not to be regarded as forms of *receiving meaning* but as forms of *giving meaning*. Going back to the basic scheme the argument here goes as follows: God has given a revelation to his believers which is to be spread. As many people as possible in the world are to live according to the revelation and must shape the world on the basis of this revelation. Fundamentalism is the extreme form of the view that the truth in its pure form is given in the foundational documents of one's own tradition – the Bible, the Qur'an- and that the world must be subjected to this truth.[8] There are however also more moderate varieties of this scheme of thought.[9] I on the other hand am of the opinion that we must make a radical break with this schema if we want to redefine the relationship of the religions with each other. For such a break it will not suffice if two or three religions turn to their respective traditions in order to find common features with other religions. If will for example not suffice if Jews, Christians and Muslims understand their own religion and those of the two others as Abrahamitic religions.[10]

The search to shape the submission under God

What is remarkable in the declaration of the Second Vatican Council about the relationship of the Church to the non-Christian religions is that first of all there is an emphasis on the way in which Muslims strive to submit whole-heartedly to God's counsel, 'just as Abraham, with whom the faith of Islam takes pleasure in linking itself, submitted to God'. On this basis the unity of Christians with Muslims and Jews as the common ancestor is discussed.[11] This, the other way round, is also the structure of the reference in the Qur'an where Abraham, Ibrahim, is presented to Jews and Christians as a shared model of faith:

> O People of the Book! [it is well known that this is the name for Jews and Christians in the Qur'an. Trough it their kinship with Islam is also expressed; E.B.] Come to a word common between us and you: that we worship none but God and shall not associate any with Him, and that we shall not take any others for lords other than God. . . . Why do you dispute about Abraham when the Torah and the Evangel were not revealed till after his time? Do you not then understand (even that much)? (Chapter 3.64' 65).

Of course, in the same way as Paul in the New Testament justifies Christianity as it has become as faithful to its origin while the competing Judaism has become unfaithful, this Islam justifies itself here by accusing Jews and Christians of having become unfaithful to Abraham and by pre-senting itself as the return to that original faith. More interesting however than the polemical reference to Abraham is the suggestion that Jews,

Christians and Muslims via Abraham might come to a shared confession of what is at the heart of their faith:

> Come to a word common between us and you: that we worship none but God and shall not associate any with Him, and that we shall not take any others for lords other than God.

Here the attempt is made to put into words a religious vision which shall accompany Jews, Christians and Muslims in their life of faith with God and thus situate them and their search for the true faith of God in the realm of God's presence. Where human beings are lords over other human beings, where something else is venerated and served as if it were God, there we, people of the book, must raise out voices, there we must oppose it and remind of the fact that there is no God apart from God.[12] Thus we witness to a lasting search for God who is true, for the truth that is divine.

Nothing is God but God alone, nothing is sacred or mighty or untouchable or of absolute importance apart from the one who is full of mercy and compassion as the Qur'an calls God. According to the Christian confession this God in his might has come closer to us than we can ever come ourselves. This God created us and journeys with us away from oppression to a land of milk and honey, freedom and abundance, as the memory of Judaism tells it. It is submission to the God who promised to Abraham a great nation and gave it, the God who seduced Abraham to a faith in an unsure and uncertain future, the God to whose will Abraham submitted, even at the potential cost of his son, his most precious possession. This is the God whom Christians and Muslims, if at all possible also in dialogue with Jews, should seek together and in doing that help each other to find him. We should be concerned with submitting to this God, not only for ourselves but also for the society in which we live. For we should not be seduced to withdraw into the private sphere by the increasing tensions between religions and religious movements on a world-wide as well as on a local level. The pressure to ban religions from public life in favour of a supposedly neutral state has been strong since the 11 September 2001, but we cannot confine God to a church or a mosque, to the Bible or the Qur'an, in our heads or in our hearts.[13] Muslims can with their conspicuous interest in shaping public life and with their urge to be manifest in public life remind Christians of precisely this.

A strict separation between the religious and private sphere is always a problem from the point of view of religion, certainly if seen from Christianity or Islam. The God who is sought by these traditions and articulated to the extent that one deems to have found traces of his presence, the God of heaven and earth whom it is impossible to exclude from particular spheres of life. From a religious point of view it is unacceptable not to speak of God's justice when we are speaking about the ordering of society, or about human beings as the image of God if we are dealing with the beginning or with the end of life, or about the mercy of God if we are speaking about politics with regard to the eradication of poverty, integrating immigrants or criminal law. Our political and social discussions would benefit if such categories were reintroduced into the public debate. Then it would become clear that the shape of the state and society is not a matter of accidental or contingent personal preferences or taste. Politics is ultimately about the questions to whom or to what we as a society want to pay homage, in which sphere of values or goods we want to situate society. With regard to the translation of religious values into a language which has meaning in the realm of the secular, I share the opinion of the German philosopher Jürgen Habermas that this is of fundamental importance in the current situation not only if we want to judge out of religious traditions but especially if our starting point is society itself.[14]

Public discussion as religious discussion

From this I draw the conclusion that Christians in their dealing with the Islamic tradition should not focus on this tradition itself. Instead they must together with Muslims on the basis of both traditions concentrate on the question as to what human beings in our society stand for, both collectively and individually. The prerogative is the assumption that God is the God of everything and of all, and that everything and everyone is thus already in a relationship with the God about whom the Christian as well as the Islamic traditions want to speak. This implies on the one hand that religions embody particular views with regard to the whole of the truth and understand them-selves as answer to a mystery which reveals itself as origin and destiny of this truth and about which one can then discuss in a reasonable and rational way. While there is no rational proof for a religious faith, it should be possible to justify it in a reasonable way, and such a critical responsibility is important, from a religious point of view. It is our religious obligation to serve God and God alone, and not an image of God which we may deem to be God, but which thus becomes an idol.

Such an iconoclasm is an important contribution of the three Abrahamic faiths to contemporary culture. Thus the question is kept alive what is indeed true, good and beautiful, and one resists modern skepticism which thinks that the true, good and beautiful cannot be recognized as such and that we can therefore not deal with anything other than an image of it. It seems that the intercultural and inter-religious dialogue in our culture is not as difficult as it is because of the differences as such but because of the current lack of faith that such a dialogue might actually lead to any kind of result. If we think that we no longer know anything about God and the will of God, then we can only discuss the relative rights of our respective different convictions. The confession that there is only one God whom we should worship reminds us that the search for truth and goodness is an inalienable right because God as the one who is true and good will not leave us behind. In this sense religious faith in no way blocks the fundamental debate about truth and goodness, about values and norms but on the contrary makes it possible and meaningful.

In these discussions everyone is included. To the extent that religions are collective convictions they separate groups and individuals from each other. To the extent however that they understand themselves as answers to the traces of God in the reality in the midst of which we human beings live, they keep alive the consciousness that we prior to all other things are interconnected with each other. We belong together before we are separated through differences with regard to viewpoints and tastes in religion and culture. The events of 11 September 2001 and everything that came after them have generated doubts in a number of different European societies with a considerable Muslim minority that a system of norms and values is possible which can unite immigrants and members of the indigenous population. From a religious point of view however this is the decisive starting point that the success and the wellbeing of allochthones and autochthones are interconnected. We inhabit the same space which is ultimately God's space, and that which happens to another challenges me to take part and to be involved – and vice versa. Christianity and Islam express their connectedness by saying that all human beings are created by God and are children of God and thus related to each other. We do not exactly know what this means, but we are searching for ways to shape this connectedness. This search we call culture, society, politics. The religious confession that we are connected with each other in God implies that religious groups and individuals have to be open for contributions to the debate and that they must not regard their own faith as the only approach to truth. God is the realm for the search for a still greater, still deeper and yet always withdrawing truth, which the religious traditions look at.

Or to put it differently: God and religion in general as well as Christianity and Islam in particular do not position themselves against the Enlightenment, even if this is frequently suggested by those who regard themselves as followers of the Enlightenment as well as by those who regard themselves as religious. God and the religions, Christianity and Islam are the space of Enlightenment.[15] Historically both religions have given space to the Enlightenment, and the challenge is to explore them again as such. It is an important theological task to help them to open themselves once again in this sense.

It is an important theological task to help them to open themselves once again in this sense.

Translated by Natalie K. Watson on the basis of the
German translation by Karel Hermans.

Notes

1. Cf for the manifold and diverse debates within contemporary Islam: Clinton Bennett, *Muslim and Modernity: An Introduction to the Issues and Debates*, London/New York, 2005.

2. As is well known, for Thomas Aquinas the starting point is that the object of theology is everything – under the aspect of God. My thesis is that this approach, in which religion is ultimately regarded as a hermeneutics of reality which must be reconstructed and critically evaluated in theology, is also the best guideline for the engaging with the confrontation with different religious traditions.

3. Cf the declaration of the Second Vatican Council about the relationship of the Church to non-Christian religions, *Nostra Aetate* (28 October 1965), 3.

4. Declaration on Religious Freedom *Dignitatis humanae* (7 December 1965), 3. http://www.vatican.va/archive/hist_councils/ii_vatican_council/documents/va t-ii_decl_19651207_dignitatis-humanae_en.html.

5. Loc. cit. 4.

6. Cf Johann Baptist Metz, 'Theologie versus Polymythie oder: Kleine Apologie des biblischen Monotheismus' in Odo Marquard/Peter Probst/Franz Josef Wetz (eds), *Einheit und Vielheit*, Hamburg, 1990, pp. 170–86; 'Im Eingedenken fremden Leids: Zu einer Basiskategorie christlicher Gottesrede' in Johann Baptist Metz./Johann Reikerstorfer/Jürgen Werblick, *Gottesrede*, Münster, 1996, pp. 3–20; *Zum Begriff der neuen politischen Theologie. 1967–1997*, Mainz 1997, pp. 197–206:

'Im Pluralismus der Religions- und Kulturwelten: Anmerkungen zu einem theolo-gisch-politischen Weltprogramm'.

7. Cf also my article '*Gaudium et Spes*: the Forgotten Future of a Revolutionary Document' *Concilium* 41 (2005/4), pp. 48 – 56.

8. According to the Egyptologist Jan Assmann (cf *Herrschaft und Heil: Politische Theologie in Altägypten, Israel und Europa*, Munich, 2000 and *Die Mosaische Unterscheidung. Oder der Preis des Monotheismus*, Munich, 2003) this logic is the basis of monotheism and of theology. Although monotheistic religions of revelation are indeed more likely to be open to this kind of logic, there is no reason to assume that there is an essential intrinsic connection between the two.

9. The emphasis of an infallible teaching as well as its autonomous development by the Roman Catholic Church since the mid nineteenth century also has to do with this scheme.

10. Cf also the article by Pim Valkenberg 'Does the Concept of 'Abrahamtic Religions' have a Future?' in this issue of *Concilium*.

11. *Nostra aetate*, 3–4

12. Cf from a Christian background Theo Witvliet, *Het geheim van het lege midden: Over de identiteit van het Westers christendom*, Zoetermeer, 2003; and from and Islamic perspective Reza Aslan, *No god but God: The Origins, Evolution, and Future of Islam*, New York, 2005.

13. Cf for the different European views about religion and public life, Church and state: John T. S. Madeley/Zsolt Enyedi (eds.), *Church and State in Contemporary Europe: The Chimera of Neutrality*, London/Portland, 2003. For the relationship between religion and politics and the debate about this, cf Pippa Norris/Ronald Inglehart, *Sacred and Secular: Religion and Politics Worldwide*, Cambridge, 2004. For the relationship between religion and democracy, see David Marquand/Ronald L. Nettler (Hg.), *Religion and Democracy*, Oxford 2000.

14. Cf Jürgen Habermas, 'Glauben und Wissen' in: *Glauben und Wissen: Friedenspreis des Deutschen Buchhandels 2001*, Frankfurt am Main, 2001, pp. 9–34.

15. This is fundamentally different from the question what space the Enlightenment has left for religion and if religion should not resist the restrictions imposed on it by the Enlightenment. Religion and the Enlightenment are connected with each other and hence the contrast between the two is secondary, something which must be understood in its origin and its concrete shapes and cannot be presupposed. In turn we can then do justice to the fact that many Enlightenment thinkers wanted to reform religion, not abolish it or push it back.

DOCUMENTATION

Islam in the Media – How it is Pictured and How it Pictures Itself

THEODORE GABRIEL

The media are a powerful agency in the modern world in the formation of public opinion. They are a powerful tool in public education and their potency cannot be underestimated. It is for this very reason that the nature of media representations, the way they go about reporting events, and discuss vital issues and the impact they have on the world have to be studied zealously. They can be an agent of good and evil, of peace and conflict.

The state of the media at present leaves much to be desired. I do not subscribe to the view that all media are sensation seekers or purveyors of sensationalism in order to sell their products, though undoubtedly there are many who go along that path. But undoubtedly there are also many who are serious, objective and try to take a balanced perspective of issues. But all are blighted by the fact that the media is a peculiar form of conveying knowledge which is immediate, terse, and not making much time for reflection or a deep study of issues. The media spotlight often moves on without giving time for the proper denouement of events or resolution of problems. Moreover the media cannot dwell on dull, commonplace or routine matters. They have to focus on trouble spots and matters of controversy. by their very objective of transmitting information to the public in an interesting way, and since they are always underwritten as a commercial venture.[1] Their very selectiveness can undermine their quest for being objective and factual. So the media representation is often not a well-studied one. The reporters are not people who have committed time to analyzing and reflecting deeply on the issues they deal with, or those who have made a thorough study of the subject matter. Thus their representation of facts runs the danger of being partial, simplistic, half true and distorted, not deliberately but inadvertently through the above stated deficiencies.

In the case of Islam the problem is compounded by the fact the media are dealing usually with cultures they are not thoroughly familiar with or about which they have no thorough or deep knowledge. Their knowledge of Islam also can be casual, superficial or even distorted. Often there are generalizations and stereotypes in presenting Islam. Terms such as *fundamentalism* and *terrorism* are banded about loosely without judging their appropriateness in a context or the full implications of such terms.

The term *fundamentalism* is of Christian provenance and essentially means one who subscribes to the literal truth of the scriptures. It has to some extent become in popular parlance synonymous with fanaticism or extremism and the media often uses the term in this way. As the perspicacious former Prime Minister of Malaysia, Dr Mahathir Muhammad once remarked, anyone who speaks of Islam in a positive way is now called a fundamentalist. It is quite inappropriate as in many media representations to use the term *fundamentalist* in a pejorative way. Douglas Pratt states: 'Here (in the West) a particular, politically nuanced meaning is loaded on to the word. In this application fundamentalism means political extremism: forms of radical fanaticisms which find direct expression and engagement in the world of every day affairs: the resurgent Islam that disrupts the status quo'.[2] The media should take the lion's share of responsibility in the misuse of this term. Similarly many people are branded as *terrorist* whereas in reality they may only be people fighting for justice and their human rights. The black people of South Africa were for long called terrorists by the apartheid regime. Israel similarly categorized Yasser Arafat and his followers as terrorists, though they were doing little else but opposing the chicanery and high handedness of the Israeli regime in evicting them from their homeland and repressing the denizens of what little land was left to them in Palestine.

The media should be sensitive to these distinctions but is often unable to do so. The term 'terrorist' has often been applied in a blanket way by the media to people who have a legitimate cause for fighting a nation or a state government. The Indian media often categorize, for example, people who fight Indian forces for obtaining freedom or autonomy of their state, as terrorists. As a matter of fact it is difficult to define what a terrorist is. Nation states may often resort to terrorism. The so called 'shock and awe' bombing tactics of the USA in the Gulf War was nothing but an act of terrorism since it was certainly intended to cause terror in the hearts of the people of Iraq.

The media often does not reflect coolly and dispassionately on the use of stereotypical terms. It is evident that since the two world wars the distinction between civilians and soldiers has become very much blurred in the context of battles and wars. High explosive bombs and incendiary devices dropped by aircraft, missiles, strafing of civilians from the air et cetera have brought the civilian populations of nations engaged in war to the battlefront. The term 'innocent civilians', often used by the media, also bears examination. In a democratic state the entire nation including civilians must share the blame for any iniquitous actions that the state government might be doing. The people who voted the government into power cannot escape responsibility. The Iraq war is generally perceived as an unprovoked, illegal assault on a sovereign nation by many. The shifting *casus belli* of this war (initially to destroy weapons of mass destruction, then to topple Saddam Hussein) indicated to many that there might have been hidden agendas, such as petroleum geopolitics or the domination of the entire Middle East behind this war. The people of Iraq, other than the cohorts of Saddam Hussein, might genuinely be described as innocent civilians in this context since they did not put Saddam Hussein into power. They were rather the long-suffering victims of a despot. But the people of the USA and the United Kingdom cannot so lightly escape responsibility. They repeatedly voted the present administrations into power. The war seemed to be an assault on Islam to many, not only to Muslims in whose psyche the war represented such an assault and were generally badly hurt by this needless war, but also to many non-Muslims. The protests in both USA and the UK and other countries bear testimony to the fact that Muslims were not alone in being offended by the Iraq war. Saddam Hussein might have been a very bad ruler, but as the great Indian leader Mahatma Gandhi once remarked, the people of a country prefer their own bad government to the good government of foreigners. The actions of the USA and the Untied Kingdom in Iraq smack of colonialism.

A country like Iraq or Palestine cannot fight a conventional war against forces vastly superior in armament, military technology and weaponry. In such contexts everywhere subjugated or oppressed people resort to unconventional forms of warfare – the human bomb is one such weapon – and to categorize all these people as terrorists falls far short of validity.

I am not here advocating the *modus operandi* of would be Muslim martyrs or *mujahideen*. Of course, political differences have to be settled by peaceful means, by negotiation or through intermediaries such as the United Nations. But in the instance of the Iraq war or the Palestinian issue negotiations were fruitless and the UN and its resolutions totally sidelined. If the United States went to war unilaterally and Israel is in breach of many United

Nations as well as other resolutions arising from peaceful negotiation such as the Oslo accord, there does not seem to be a propensity to engage in peaceful resolutions to problems. They seem to be unduly convinced of the infallibility of coercion, and like begets like. One can therefore empathize with suicide bombers who set out to attack Israel and the coalition of Western nations in Iraq. The fact is that these *mujahideen* are not seasoned killers or those who relish violence, as some of the protagonists in Northern Ireland seem to be, but individuals who are deeply religious and mostly novices in the art of warfare and violence.

The fact is that justice has been the victim in both Iraq and Israel. The people of the offending nations also bear responsibility and cannot escape their collective burden of having put the governments of their nations into power. Thus acts which are defined as terrorism can also be interpreted as legitimate warfare. At the least the suffering of civilians might be, as the US jargon puts it, collateral damage.

The reporter who put together the recent BBC Panorama presentation on Islamic terrorism failed to be sensitive enough to reflect on these issues. He tried to browbeat the Secretary of the Islamic Council of Britain and failed to understand that this intelligent individual, Mr. Iqbal Sacranie, was trying to make a distinction between people who had a legitimate grievance for adopting violent actions and those who do it for purely violence *qua* violence. This programme is a model for very insensitive ham fisted journalism.

The truth of the matter is that western reporting, while claiming to be fair and objective, often displays tinges of being defensive of the policies of their nation states. This is almost subconscious, the media often posing to be very critical of the administration of their own nations and the champion of the underdogs. However, the selectiveness of their presentation and the coverage on the whole presents a case that is favourable to the policymakers in their own countries. This was brought home to me forcefully when I consulted the Iraq war coverage of Egyptian and Indian media, nations that are in no way biased or hostile to the West, and found much there that was not presented in the Western media, and was unfavourable to the actions and policies of the USA. I concur with Edward Said in his well-studied work *Covering Islam*. He states:

> It (the western Media) has given consumers of news the sense that they have understood Islam without at the same time intimating to them that a great deal in this coverage is based on far from objective material. In many

instances 'Islam' has licensed not only patent inaccuracy but also expressions of unrestrained ethno-centrism, cultural and even racial hatred, deep yet paradoxically free-floating hostility. All this has taken place as part of what is presumed to be fair, balanced, responsible coverage of Islam.[3]

Islam has a bad image now as a violent, militant and intransigent religion mainly due to the media focus on the trouble spots of the Islamic world and the actions of fanatics and those who resort to violence for the redressal of issues. This is a total distortion of the truth. The media have made Islam known to the world, but what it has revealed is not an authentic Islam. Of course, there are passages in the Qur'an that seem to sanction violence but the meaning of these passages is not as obvious as thought, and they bear careful examination and interpretation and reference to the contexts in which the revelations were received.[4] Moreover, there are similar passages in every scripture. The Old Testament shows how God commanded a total massacre of men, women, children and animals to King Saul.[5] In the Bhagavad Gita the god Krishna advocates war to the recalcitrant warrior Arjuna. Even in pacifist religions such as Christianity and Buddhism there have been institutions such as the Crusaders and warrior monks. In a perceptive article John Shepherd writes: 'The issue of moral criteria of religious truth is critical to the ever more urgent task of rendering religions safe for human consumption.'[6] Thus there is no need for the media to subscribe to the popular notion of Islam as a violent religion or to single it out in this context. But often the media approach to events seems to underwrite this false notion.

The media often fails to recognize the diversity of Islam. It tends to present Islam as a monolithic entity and to consider that all Muslims are essentially ideologically identical and to possess a common attitude and approach to issues. This is a totally false notion. Part of this fallacy occurs with the concept of the Islamic Ummah. It is true that in comparison to many faiths Islam might have lesser sectarianism and denominationalism. Islam might engender greater solidarity. But this never negates the fact that there is a diversity of opinion and ideology in the global Islamic community. This sort of false conceptualization has branded Islam as a menace to the world and tarred all Muslims with the same brush. Part of the problem is the propensity of some Western scholars and politicians to see Islam as the new enemy after the fall of Communism. The demonization of Islam is growing apace. Bush and Tony Blair often talk of the clash of civilizations and ways of life. There are people they aver (meaning inevitably Muslims) bent upon destroying our culture, values and ways of life. They have both specifically declared that Islam is not the enemy. Yet Islam has been used to demonize enemies, or rather victims of Western hegemony and political intrusion into affairs of state in Islamic lands in the only ways that they can against power-ful states. Elizabeth Poole points out that the media has played a role in constructing the idea in popular psychic imagination that September 11th represents a rupture and a new world order must be established conse-quently.[7] Poole continues, stating that the media focussed on the build up to military action rather than alternative solutions thereby creating the expectation and acceptance of war.[8]

How Muslims see themselves

Islam is a religion that has transcended barriers of race, language, national borders and to some extent culture. Though of late there is a reversion to the 'Arab idea' in Islam prompted by the Wahabi- Salafi factions which extol the original Islam of the Prophet's days and would tend to decry the develop-ments over the centuries which has made it multicultural by allowing for the cultural osmosis and adaptations in its manifestations in non-Arab lands, Islam embraces a rich diversity of traditions, cultures and ways of life. The five pillars of Islam, the *Ibadah*, and the respect and desire to conform with in which Sharia Islamic law is held though not often binding on all Muslims, especially in secularly minded Muslim nations, has ensured a certain homo-geneity in religious and social practice. Muslims are proud of their religious identity and are conscious that they are a vast chunk of the world population (one billion and one fifth of the world population). Most Muslims cherish their religion, and though they may all not conform to its edicts or may even not be practicing strictly all the daily and seasonal religious duties incumbent on them as Muslims, yet respect and have an affinity with their identity as Muslims and with fellow Muslims of all kinds. They look upon their faith as simple and straight foreword, and have mostly always stayed clear of complex theological formulations, though this does not mean that Islam does not possess or have scope for detailed theological discussions and conceptualisation. 'There is no god but God and Muhammad is his prophet' sets the seal of Islam for them upon themselves and their co-religionists. Not all Muslims wear their religion on their sleeve as is commonly imagined. The bearded skullcap and flowing robe wearing Muslim male and the *hijab* or *abhaya* wearing Muslim woman is a stereotype and one can find numerous exemptions to this image of Islam among Muslims of the world.

As Esposito states, Islam and Islamic movements may well be seen as a threat (a green menace in place of the red menace of communism) or a challenge or potential danger by Christianity and the West.[9] But this is currently not a perception that Muslims will hold of themselves or will acquiesce to. To themselves the vast majority of Muslims are peaceful and desiring a quiet and a happy life free to practise life as they cherish as good servants (*abd*) of Allah. To a minority of fanatics or extremists there are millions upon millions of peace-loving Muslims in the world, leading normal lives, be they in Pakistan or Malaysia or Iraq. The images of Muslim mothers bewailing the death of their children, husbands or close family is a harrowing sight on our TV screens ever since the arising of the Palestine problem and the Iraq war and show them to be normal, and vulnerable to the vagaries of fortune as any one else.

To be liked is a human propensity and Muslims are no exception to this. They also prefer to be liked rather than hated or feared as a threat or danger. My Indian friends domiciled in the Persian Gulf state that their Arab employers are very likeable and were hardly a threat to them. This does note mean that they will not react to injustice. When I taught in the Muslim Indian territory of the Lakshadweep Islands one of the first things that my more experienced colleagues told me was to treat the people there with justice and if possible with affection. Their liking and support for us will then be assured my colleagues used to say.

Muslims, I often feel, have a more ready consciousness of being subject to the will of God than the followers of other faiths. Inshallah (If God wills) is a favourite saying among them. There is a general consciousness that God's will is paramount. All Muslims may not tread the *sirat al musthuqin*, the straight and narrow path, but most will desire to. The structure of their religious practice is designed to make them feel the presence of God throughout their daily life and in the seasons. In times of trial and tribulation their faith in God is something for them to turn to and get a feeling of comfort and support. Few Muslims can be so alienated from their faith that they become totally secular. This is what a Muslim who is not particularly devout or observant of rituals which he sometimes finds too repetitive and ritualistic. He states: 'I get comfort in submission to Allah and thank Him for his bounty . . . If living in a secular society means not recognising these gifts of God then I don't want to live in such a society.'[10]

I hope that in this short article I have been able to illuminate the Muslim world view and point out deficiencies in contemporary media representations of Islam which have been extremely damaging to the image of the faith, a perversion of the truth, and has contributed to the general misapprehension that it is an aggressive, militant and violence-prone faith.

Notes

1. The BBC has no profit making objective yet it still has to satisfy the general public who fund the organization thorough a television licence fee and has thus to compete for viewers with the commercial channels

2. Douglas Pratt, *The Challenge of Islam,* Aldershot, Ashgate, 2005, p. 183.

3. Edward Said, *Covering Islam*, London, Routledge, 1981.

4. For instance Qur'an 2.191.

5. 1 Samuel 15.3.

6. John Shepherd, 'Self- Critical Children of Abraham?' in Gabriel, T, et al, (eds), *Islam and the West Post- September 11th*, Aldershot, Ashgate, 2004, p. 42.

7. Elizabeth Poole, *Reporting Islam*, New York, IB Tauris, 2002, p. 2.

8. Ibid.; p. 3.

9. John L. Esposito, *The Islamic Threat: Myth or Reality?* New York, Oxford University Press, 1999, p. 3.

10. Mohammed A. Khan, 'I am a Muslim' in Christopher Partridge (ed.), *The Lion Handbook of The World's Religions*, Oxford, Lion Hudson PLC, 2005, p. 390.

Religious Reactions and Initiatives after the Terrorist Attacks in London, July 2005

LUCINDA ORY

Four suicide bombers struck in central London on Thursday 7 July 2005, killing more than 50 people and injuring at least 700. The co-ordinated attacks hit the transport system as the morning rush hour drew to a close. The attacks were claimed by Al-Queda (Arabic: 'the base'), an international Muslim terrorist network. On 21 July of this year radical Muslims once again attacked the British capital. Nobody got killed, but these attacks had a huge emotional impact on the British people.

The same day the first series of attacks took place, prime minister Tony Blair declared he feared aggressive anti-Muslim feelings, which, as he said, would do no right to the peaceful majority of Muslims living in his country. The amount of crimes which had to do with 'religious hate against Muslims' in London indeed rapidly increased after the attacks.

Here, some reactions to these events and initiatives are presented, coming from a religious background, both Christian and Muslim.

After the bombings Church leaders quickly started working with Muslim organizations to ensure that their congregations are united against any possible anti-Islamic backlash. Sir Iqbal Sacranie, head of the Muslim Council of Britain (an umbrella body with over 400 affiliated national, regional and local organizations, mosques, charities and schools) said he utterly condemned the attacks. 'These terrorists, these evil people, want to demoralize us as a nation and divide us.' He admitted 'there may well be elements who want to exploit this tragedy and incite hatred.'

And the Bishop of Stepney, Stephen Oliver, and Dr Mohammed Abdul Bari, the Chairman of the East London Mosque, spoke together outside the Royal London Hospital saying the East End and London must remain united in the face of terror. Dr Bari said: 'We're just shocked and horrified by what has happened. I spoke to the congregation at the mosque and tried to calm their fears and told them they must remain vigilant. We have worked together with the communities in the East End for many years and we must continue doing so.' Bishop Oliver said: 'When something like this happens people are at first afraid, and then people get angry. There's a great deal of speculation in this atmosphere. We are determined that whatever the reaction it is one that unites the different faith communities.'

Churches and other faith groups in multi-ethnic areas of Britain made an approach and spoke out in support of the Muslim community to ensure that community relations are not damaged as a result of the radical Islamist involvement in the bombings. Among those who have spoken out in support of their Islamic neighbours are the diocesan and area bishops of the Anglican Diocese of Lichfield. Before a service of Evensong at Lichfield Cathedral where prayers were said for all those caught up in the attacks, Jonathan Gledhill, Bishop of Lichfield, said: 'Living near most of us will be families who are quite worried that they may be identified with a terror attack simply because they are from another faith. I want us to do what we can to reassure them that we recognize that just as the IRA has nothing to do with Christianity; so this kind of terror has nothing to do with any of the world faiths.'

His sentiments were echoed by Dr Alan Smith, Bishop of Shrewsbury, who said: 'Now that a website has been found claiming that the London bombings were undertaken by an Islamic group, it is vitally important that we speak out against any people in our own country who might use this as an excuse for racist attacks.'

In Wolverhampton yesterday evening, prayers were said for the City of London and its people and all those caught up in the 7 July bombings, at a service in the Anglican St Peter's Church in the centre of the city. Introducing the service, the Rector of Wolverhampton, David Frith, said: 'This is a simple service of grief and hope as we bring to mind the events of the day. This is not a time to focus on the evil that has been perpetrated. That evil is not worthy of our attention.' Afterwards the Bishop of Wolverhampton was joined by members of the Wolverhampton Interfaith Group who issued a united condemnation of the attacks and offered their condolences for those affected by the atrocity.

Michael Bourke, President of the Wolverhampton Interfaith Group, said: 'All our faiths unite in condemning utterly this indiscriminate mass murder. If it turns out that these crimes were motivated in any way by religion, we utterly denounce such religion as having nothing to do with God our creator, our judge, our redeemer and our hope.' He went on: 'The Christian faith forbids revenge. We therefore offer our complete support to people of any faith or none who may be the target of attacks or threats as a result of this events.'

Another initiative was made by the Muslim Council of Britain and Churches Together in Britain and Ireland, an umbrella organization for the mainstream Christian denominations. They delivered a joint statement on the terrorist attacks. Both sides condemned the attacks 'in the strongest possible terms'. 'No good purpose can be achieved by such an indiscriminate and cruel use of terror.' They also stated that 'the scriptures and the traditions of both the Muslim and Christian communities repudiate the use of such violence. Religious precepts cannot be used to justify such crimes, which are completely contrary to our teaching and practice. We continue to resist all attempts to associate our communities with the hateful acts of any minority who claim falsely to represent us. In the present uncertainties, we look to all community leaders to give an example of wisdom, tolerance and compassion.'

And: 'The events of recent years have challenged Muslims and Christians to work together in order to acknowledge our differences, to affirm our common humanity and to seek ways to share life together. Much has already been achieved and nothing must undermine the progress that we have made. These attacks strengthen our determination to live together in peace and to grow together in mutual understanding.'

In the wake of the London bombings Anglicans and Muslims took the initiative to a new 'Forum of Muslims and Christians' which is going to be launched in 2006. Bishop Austin spent three years investigating the creation of the forum and last year Bishop David Gillett brought together a working party of Christians and Muslims to put the proposals into action. The new forum will have difficult issues to tackle on extremism and the place of violence in Islamist theology. Many Christians will also be urgently asking the forum to tackle the lack of rights given to Christian minorities in over-whelmingly Muslim societies. But it is thought the Forum will also work towards identifying areas of common action which can be found in the area of ethics, fighting poverty and combating racism. The Archbishop of Canterbury, Dr Rowan Williams, is to head the forum and there will be four Christian and four Muslim Presidents. Muslim leaders are likely to be senior Imams from British cities. A problem the forum faces is in whether it will be regarded as authoritative and representative in the diverse Muslim community. Many senior Muslim Imams who could be considered for the Forum are moderately 'Islamist', while very few prominent leaders represent the Sufi or Shi'ite traditions, for example. Muslims have not had a recognized national religious leadership and the four Muslim Presidents of the forum are to be senior Imams, rather than leaders of lobbying groups such as the Muslim Council of Britain.

Another rapprochement to the Muslim community came from the Anglican Bishop of Bangor, Anthony Crockett, and the Dean of Bangor, Alun Hawkins. They invited Moroccan-born policeman and religious leader Mohammed al-Arabi Lachiri to take the pulpit during a service at Bangor Cathedral in September 2005. It is believed it was the first time in the cathedral's centuries-old history (the first church was established in Bangor in the sixth century) that a Muslim took part in a service.

The invitation to take part in the cathedral service came after senior Bangor clergy and members of the cathedral congregation attended the Islamic Friday prayers at the Bangor mosque, just 24 hours after the London terrorist attacks, to show their support to the local Muslim community. Representatives delivered an invitation to the Islamic Centre and they were delighted when it was accepted. The Dean of Bangor said: 'PC al-Arabi Lachri will take part in our full service procession and will be allocated the 15 to 20 minute sermon slot to say whatever he likes. It is a way of offering our support to the Islamic community and of showing understanding and unity at a difficult time.'

Al-Arabi Lachiri, also deputy chairman of the Muslim Council in North Wales, said there are many similarities between the Muslim and Anglican faiths. He added: 'We both call for peace and wish to live in harmony. Both faiths want to work together for a better future. I have not decided exactly what I shall say during my address but I hope to clarify some misunderstandings about the Muslim faith.'

Another multi-faith gathering took place at Stoke Minster, exactly 24 hours after the London bombings. Religious leaders from all faiths gathered in a show of unity, keen to avoid any backlash against Muslims. The Imam of Shelton joined the Anglican Archdeacon; the Hebrew Congregation stood shoulder to shoulder with the Roman Catholic Church; the Hindus alongside the Methodists. One of the organisers, Keith Perrin (who co-ordinates the North Staffordshire Forum of Faiths), said it was a chance for people from different religions to come together to condemn the bombings.

On the part of the Catholic Church the leader of Catholics in England and

Wales made an appeal to Christians to sympathize with oppressed Muslims in a bid to combat Islamic extremists. In his speech, to a gathering in Lyon in September 2005, Cardinal Cormac Murphy-O'Connor said the 7 July bombers may have felt a sense of alienation due to being 'left hanging' between their Asian ancestry and British upbringing. 'Rejecting both, they fell vulnerable to a version of Arabic Islam which sees fit to interpret the Qur'an in isolation from the interpretative communities and legislative traditions of the faith. This ideology fuelled their fury at injustice and offered them a way of overcoming it, one that they were persuaded to believe could please God by sacrificing themselves and others in the process.' The Cardinal said defending religious freedom was crucial in ensuring newly assimilated groups felt welcome in society and he also said the alienation of Muslim youth needed to be addressed.

A lot of Muslim organizations, next to the ones discussed earlier, spoke of their sorrow. For instance the Islamic Society of Britain with its president, Munir Ahmed, urging people to 'keep alive the Olympic spirit . . . terrorism will not defeat us' (ISB). In similar fashion, the UK Islamic Mission dis-associated itself completely from any organization, claiming to be Muslim or otherwise, that carries out acts contrary to the teachings of Islam: peace, justice, freedom and the love of humanity (UKIM). In mosques across the country, imams took the opportunity of Friday prayers to condemn the bombings and to tell their congregations that they had no reason to be ashamed but should go about their daily lives as usual. Azad Ali, chairman of the Muslim Safety Forum, where Islamic leaders and senior police officers meet to discuss the policing of terrorism and other issues, has reinforced this point by saying that, while he was happy with the way that the police were handling hate crime so far, the media was not being helpful when it used terms like 'Islamic terrorist'. Instead, he called on them to stick to what the police were saying, that the bombings were the work of criminals: in his view, everyone needed to remember that 'crimes are committed by individuals, not communities'.

Contributors

ASMA ASFARUSSIN is associate professor of Arabic and Islamic Studies at the University of Notre Dame. Her fields of research are Islamic political and religious thought, Qur'an and *hadith*, Islamic intellectual history, and gender issues. She is the author or editor of three books, the most recent being *Excellence and Precedence: Medieval Islamic Discourse on Legitimate Leadership* (Leiden, 2002). She has also written over fifty articles and essays on various aspects of Islamic thought and has lectured extensively in the United States and abroad. She previously taught at Harvard University and is currently a member of the editorial boards of the *Oxford Encyclopedia of Modern Islam* and the *Routledge Encyclopedia of the Qur'an*. Afsaruddin's research has been funded by the Harry Frank Guggenheim Foundation, among others, and she was recently named a Carnegie Scholar for 2005 by the Carnegie Corporation of New York.

Address: 341 Decio Hall, University of Notre Dame, Notre Dame, IN 46556, USA
E-mail: afsaruddin.1@nd.edu

ERIK P.N.M BORGMAN has been director of the Heyerdaal Instituut of the Radboud University in Nijmegen, an inter-disciplinary research institute for theology, science and culture, since 2004. His current research interests are primarily in the area of the cultural and theological significance of contemporary culture. In this area he published a number of scholarly and popular articles; a collection of essays *Alexamenos aanbidt zijn God* (Zoetermeer 1994); *Dominicaanse spiritualiteit: Een verkenning*, in Tijdschrift *voor Geestelijk Leven* (Leuven/Berg en Dal 2000; English translation: *Dominican Spirituality: An Exploration*, London/New York 2002). Borgman is editorial secretary of the *Tijdschrift voor Theologie* and a director of *Concilium*.

His most recent contribution to *Concilium* wa '*Gaudium et Spes*: the Forgotten Future of a Revolutionary Document' (2005/4).

Address: Heyendaal Instituut, Erasmusplein 1, NL-6525 HT Nijmegen, Netherlands.
E-Mail: E.Borgman@hin.ru.nl

NELLY VAN DOORN-HARDER has been teaching world religions since 1999 at Valparaiso University, IN., USA. Since 2004 she has also been connected to the Vrije Universiteit in Amsterdam as Chair for Muslim-Christian Dialogue. Before joining Valparaiso University, she taught Islamic Studies at Duta Wacana University in Yogyakarta, Indonesia. Based on fieldwork completed during the years there she wrote a book called *Women Shaping Islam. Indonesian Muslim Women Reading the Qur'an* (University of Illinois Press, forthcoming 2006). Apart from her work on Indonesian Islam, she is a specialist on Coptic Orthodox Christianity in Egypt and has published widely on Coptic monasticism, the role of women, and on a variety of contemporary Coptic topics. Some of her books about the Copts are: *Contemporary Coptic Nuns* (1995), and with Kari Vogt, *Between Desert and City: the Coptic Orthodox Church Today* (1997).

Address: 1805 Washington Street, Valparaiso, IN 46383, USA.
E-mail: haaften123@hotmail.com

THEODORE GABRIEL graduated in Sociology and Anthropology in India and did postgraduate research work in Social Anthropology and Religious Studies at the University of Aberdeen, graduating with MLitt and PhD in 1982 and 1986 respectively. He had previously worked in the Education Department of the Muslim Indian territory of Lakshadweep for 15 years. He thereafter taught Islam at the universities of Aberdeen and Gloucestershire till the year 2000. He is now Emeritus Senior Lecturer and Honorary Research Fellow at the University of Gloucestershire. He is the author of *Lakshadweep, History, Religion and Society* (1987), *Hindu- Muslim Relations in North Malabar, 1498–1947* (1996), *Christian-Muslim Relations, a case study of Sarawak, East Malaysia,* (1996), and *Hindu and Muslim Inter-Religous Relations in Malaysia,* (2000). He was also Editor of *Islam in the*

Contemporary World (2000) and co- editor of *Mysticisms East and West*, (2004) and *Islam and the West Post- September the 11th* (2005).

Address: University of Gloucestershire, Francis Close Campus, Cheltenham, GL50 4AZ, United Kingdom.

MARC DE KESEL teaches philosophy at *Arteveldehogeschool Gent* (Belgium) and is as senior researcher affiliated to the *Radboud Universiteit* Nijmegen and the *Jan van Eyck Academy*, Maastricht (both in the Netherlands). Most of his writings concern continental philosophy (Bataille, Lefort, Derrida, Lacan, et al.). He is now preparing an English translation of his book on Lacan's seminar on ethics: 'Eros & Ethics: Reading Jacques Lacan, *Séminaire VII*' (forthcoming).

Address: Radboud Universiteit, Heyendaal Instituut, Erasmusplein 1 (19.18), P.O. Box 9103, NL – 6500 HD Nijmegen, Netherlands.
E-mail: M.deKesel@hin.ru.nl

HANS KÜNG, born 1928 in Sursee (Switzerland). 1948–1957 philosophical and theological studies at the Gregorian University, the Sorbonne and the Institut Catholique de Paris. 1962–1965 official theological consultant (*Peritus*) to the Second Vatican Council appointed by Pope John XXIII. 1960–1963 Professor of Fundamental Theology, 1963–80 Professor of Dogmatic and Ecumenical Theology at the Faculty of Catholic Theology and Director of the Institute for Ecumenical Research at the University of Tübingen; since 1980 Professor of Ecumenical Theology and Director of the Institute for Ecumenical Research at the University of Tübingen. 1996 Professor emeritus and President of the Foundation for a Global Ethic (Weltethos). Honorary Degrees from several universities.

Küng is coeditor of several journals and has written many books, including *Justification, The Council and Reunion, The Church, Infallible?, On Being a Christian, Does God Exist?, Eternal Life?, Christianity and the World Religions, Theology for the Third Millennium, Christianity and the Chinese Religions*, Reforming the Church Today, *Global Responsibility, Judaism, Credo, Great Christian Thinkers, Christianity, "A Dignified Dying"* (together with Prof. Walter Jens), *Global Ethics for Global Politics and Economics* (1997), *The Catholic Church. A Short History* (2001), *Der Islam. Geschichte,*

Gegenwart, Zukunft (2004). Co-editor: *A Global Ethic. The Declaration of the Parliament of the World's Religions.* Editor: *Yes to a Global Ethic.*

Address: Waldhauserstrasse 23, D-72076 Tübingen, Germany.

LUCINDA ORY, studied Journalism and has a BA in Religion Studies. She is currently studying for her Master 's degree in Inter-Faith Spirituality at the Radboud University Nijmegen.

MARCEL J.H.M. POORTHUIS was born in 1955 in Hilversum and studied until 1973 Theology and Judaica. H is doctorate was about the Jewish philosopher Emmanuel Levinas. Subsequently he completed a music degree at the conservatorium at Hilversum. At the moment he is the coordinator of the research project 'Relations between Judaism and Christianity' at the Katholieke Theologische Universiteit in Utrecht and lecturer for the Master's programme Inter-religious dialogue. He is co-editor of the international *Jewish and Christian Perspectives* (Brill, Leiden) and one of the co-editors of the publication The three rings. Textual studies in the historical trialogue of Judaism, Christianity and Islam (Leuven 2005). He publishes about philosophy, Judaism and early Christianity.

Address: Katholieke Theologische Universiteit te Utrecht, Heidelberglaan 2, 3584 CS Utrecht, Netherlands.
Email: mpoorthuis@ktu.nl

PIM (DR W.G.B.M.) VALKENBERG (1954) is Assistant Professor of Dogmatic Theology and the Theology of Religions at the Faculty of Theology, Radboud University, Nijmegen. His main fields of interest are Christology and Trinitarian theology, theologies of religions in Abrahamic religions, and comparative Islamo-Christian theology. His main publications include: *The Polemical Dialogue: Research into Dialogue, Truth, and Truthfulness* (Saarbrücken 1997); *Begaanbare wegen: christologie en interreligieuze dialoog* (Kampen 1998); *Words of the Living God: Place and Function of Holy Scripture in the Theology of St. Thomas Aquinas* (Leuven 2000); *God en geweld* (Budel 2002); *In de voetsporen van Abraham* (Budel 2004), *The Three Rings: Textual Studies in the historical trialogue of Judaism, Christianity and Islam* (Leuven 2005), *Sharing Lights on the Way to God: Muslim-Christian dialogue and theology in the context of Abrahamic partnership* (Amsterdam – New York, in press).

Address: De Geerkamp 14–22, 6545 HL Nijmegen, Netherlands.
E-mail: p.valkenberg@theo.ru.nl

KAREN VINTGES is a Senior Lecturer in Political and Social Philosophy in the Department of Philosophy at the University of Amsterdam. She has published *Philosophy as Passion. The Thinking of Simone de Beauvoir* (Bloomington: Indiana University Press, 1996 [originally in Dutch, 1992]); *Feminism and the Final Foucault* (with D.Taylor, Illinois University Press, 2004) and several other books in Dutch. She was a founder and editor of the Dutch journal *Krisis* and *inter alia* organized the conference 'Women and Islam: New Perspectives' which took place in Amsterdam in May 2005. She is currently working on a project entitled *Rewriting* The Second Sex *from a Global Perspective*.

Address: Nieuwe Doelenstraat 15, 1012 CP Amsterdam.

THEO W.A. DE WIT was born in 1953 and studied theology and philosophy Nijmegen. Since 1986 he is university lecturer in social political philosophy and cultural philosophy connected with the Katholieke Theologische Universiteit in Utrecht. He wrote a thesis about the political philosophy Carl Schmitt (*De onontkoombaarheid van de politiek*, Nijmegen 1992) and regularly publishes on on social ethical and political philosophical subjects. In recent years he co-edited *Solidariteit. Filosofische kritiek, ethiek en politiek* (Amsterdam, 1999), *De ordening van het verlangen* (Zoetermeer, 1999), *Gevoel zonder grenzen. Authentiek leven, medelijden en sentimentaliteit* (Nijmegen, 2000), *De nieuwe achteloosheid* (Kampen 2001), *Humanisme en Religie* (Delft 2005). His current research interests are democracy and power, politics and religion, and multiculturalism and tolerance.

Address: Alexander Numankade 41, 3572 KR Utrecht, Netherlands.
E-mail: tdewit@ktu.nl

CONCILIUM

FOUNDERS

A. van den Boogaard
P. Brand
Y. Congar OP †
H. Küng
J.-B. Metz
K. Rahner SJ †
E. Schillebeeckx OP

FOUNDATION

Jan Peters SJ (President)
Paul Vos (Treasurer)
Erik Borgman
Alberto Melloni
Susan Ross
Felix Wilfred

DIRECTORS

Regina Ammicht-Quinn (Frankfurt, Germany)
Erik Borgman (Nijmegen, The Netherlands)
Christophe Boureux OP (Lyon, France)
Eamonn Conway (Limerick, Ireland)
Hille Haker (Frankfurt, Germany)
Diego Irarrazaval (Santiago, Chile)
Maureen Junker-Kenny (Dublin, Ireland)
Solange Lefevbre (Montreal, Canada)
Alberto Melloni (Reggio Emilia, Italy)
Eloi Messi Metogo (Yaoundé, Cameroun)
Susan Ross (Chicago, USA)
Janet Martin Soskice (Cambridge, UK)
Jon Sobrino SJ (San Salvador, El Salvador)
Luiz Carlos Susin (Porto Alegre, Brazil)
Andrés Torres Queiruga (Santiago de Compostela, Spain)
Marie-Theres Wacker (Münster, Germany)
Elaine Wainwright (Auckland, New Zealand)
Felix Wilfred (Madras, India)

General Secretariat: Erasmusplein 1, 6525 HT Nijmegen, The Netherlands
http://www.concilium.org
Manager: Baroness Christine van Wijnbergen

Concilium Subscription Information

February   2006/1: *A Time of Change: Open Questions*

April   2006/2: *Theology in a World of Specialization*

June   2006/3: *Feminism in Religions*

October   2006/4: *African Christianities*

December   2006/5: *Resurrection*

New subscribers: to receive *Concilium 2005* (five issues) anywhere in the world, please copy this form, complete it in block capitals and send it with your payment to the address below.

Please enter my subscription for *Concilium 2006*

Individuals	Institutions
____ £35.00 UK/Rest of World	____ £48.50 UK/Rest of World
____ $67.00 North America	____ $93.50 North America
____ €60.00	____ €80.00.50

Please add £17.50/$33.50/€30 for airmail delivery

Payment Details:
Payment must accompany all orders and can be made by cheque or credit card
I enclose a cheque for £/$ _____ Payable to SCM-Canterbury Press Ltd
Please charge my Visa/MasterCard (Delete as appropriate) for £/$ _____
Credit card number ....
Expiry date ....
Signature of cardholder ....
Name on card ....
Telephone .... E-mail ....

Send your order to *Concilium*, SCM-Canterbury Press Ltd
9–17 St Albans Place, London N1 ONX, UK
Tel +44 (0)20 7359 8033 Fax +44 (0)20 7359 0049
E-Mail: office@scm-canterburypress.co.uk

Customer service information:
All orders must be prepaid. Subscriptions are entered on an annual basis (i.e. January to December) No refunds on subscriptions will be made after the first issue of the Journal has been despatched. If you have any queries or require information about other payment methods, please contact our Customer services department.